UNDERSTANDING
GARY SNYDER

Understanding Contemporary
American Literature

Matthew J. Bruccoli, *Editor*

UNDERSTANDING
Gary
SNYDER

PATRICK D. MURPHY

UNIVERSITY OF SOUTH CAROLINA PRESS

Published in Columbia, South Carolina, by the
University of South Carolina Press

Manufactured in the United States of America

Library of Congress Cataloging-in-Publication Data

Murphy, Patrick D., 1951–
    Understanding Gary Snyder / by Patrick D. Murphy.
       p.   cm.—(Understanding contemporary American literature)
    Includes bibliographical references (p.) and index.
    ISBN 0–87249–821–2 (hard back : acid free)
    1. Snyder, Gary—Criticism and interpretation. I. Title.
  II. Series.
  PS3569.N88Z79   1992   91–46461
  811'.54—dc20

For

Bonnie Iwasaki-Murphy

Katsunori Yamazato

Eric Paul Shaffer

For what each has contributed to my

participation in the work of cultural transmission

CONTENTS

Editor's Preface   ix

Preface   xi

Acknowledgments   xiii

Chapter 1   "True Voyage is Return":
Career and Overview   1

Chapter 2   From Myth Criticism to Mythopoeia:
Myths & Texts   21

Chapter 3   Working Rhythms:
Riprap & Cold Mountain Poems   43

Chapter 4   Of Mountains, Rivers, and Back Country:
*Six Sections from Mountains and Rivers
without End Plus One* and *The Back
Country*   65

Chapter 5   The Waves of Household and Marriage:
Earth House Hold and *Regarding
Wave*   92

Chapter 6   Reinhabiting the Land:
Turtle Island, *The Old Ways*, and *Passage
Through India*   109

Chapter 7   Handing Down the Practice: *Axe Handles*
and *Left Out in the Rain*   134

Contents

Chapter 8   Of Wildness and Wilderness in Plain
            Language: *The Practice of the Wild*   154

Conclusion   167

Bibliography   171

Index   179

EDITOR'S PREFACE

Understanding Contemporary American Literature has been planned as a series of guides or companions for students as well as good nonacademic readers. The editor and publisher perceive a need for these volumes because much of the influential contemporary literature makes special demands. Uninitiated readers encounter difficulty in approaching works that depart from the traditional forms and techniques of prose and poetry. Literature relies on conventions, but the conventions keep evolving; new writers form their own conventions—which in time may become familiar. Put simply, *UCAL* provides instruction in how to read certain contemporary writers—identifying and explicating their material, themes, use of language, point of view, structures, symbolism, and responses to experience.

The word *understanding* in the series title was deliberately chosen. Many willing readers lack an adequate understanding of how contemporary literature works; that is, what the author is attempting to express and the means by which it is conveyed. Although the criticism and analysis in the series have been aimed at a level of general accessibility, these introductory volumes are meant to be applied in conjunction with the works they cover. Thus they do not provide a substitute for the works and authors they introduce, but rather prepare the reader for more profitable literary experiences.

M.J.B.

PREFACE

Gary Snyder is an extremely active, multifaceted, and complex poet, social activist, and personality. I have attempted to fulfill the goals of this series by providing an introduction to Snyder's career, key influences, and all of his full-length published volumes. These volumes include poetry and prose and are presented roughly in the order of their publication, with a few exceptions where I thought the time of composition took precedence for interpretation. Rather than congesting the text with passing references, I have limited myself to citing those works that shed particularly pertinent insights on Snyder's writing and which have been most influential on the shaping of my own interpretations.

Many people and institutions have facilitated my work on this book, and I would like to acknowledge their assistance. I am indebted to the State System of Higher Education of Pennsylvania for its generosity in providing me with a faculty research grant for the fall of 1990 and to the Graduate School of Indiana University of Pennsylvania for assisting me with the development of that grant proposal. My graduate research assistant at IUP, Mark Noon, aided me with his professional and efficient handling of numerous duties. Brother Nick Koss deserves thanks for inviting me to Fu Jen University, Taipei, Taiwan, in the fall of 1990 to participate in a conference that focused in part on Gary Snyder. And I thank the University of California, Davis, Research Library Special Collections Department, particularly John Skarstad, for not only enabling my study of the Gary Snyder Archives there but also granting me permission to quote from some of that material.

Dialogue with several Snyder critics, such as Dave Robertson, Katsunori Yamazato, Eric Shaffer, and Julia Martin, helped me prepare to write this book. Julia Martin particularly helped by critiquing several chapters of the manuscript. Finally, I would like to thank the two most important people for this project:

Bonnie Iwasaki-Murphy who provided very specific as well as indefinable support and Gary Snyder who has been both source and critic. He made invaluable comments on the manuscript and granted me permission to quote from unpublished material in and out of the archives at Davis and from published material as well.

ACKNOWLEDGMENTS

Quotations from published and unpublished materials in the Gary Snyder Archives are used by permission of the Department of Special Collections, University of California Library, Davis, California.

Quotations from *Six Sections from Mountains and Rivers without End, Plus One* are used by permission of Four Seasons Foundation.

Quotations from *Riprap*, copyright ©1965, and *Axe Handles*, copyright ©1983 by Gary Snyder, are reprinted by permission of North Point Press.

Quotations from Gary Snyder: *Myths & Texts*, copyright ©1960, 1978, by Gary Snyder; Gary Snyder: *The Back Country*, copyright ©1957, 1968 by Gary Snyder; and Gary Snyder: *Turtle Island*, copyright ©1974 by Gary Snyder are all reprinted by permission of New Directions Publishing Corporation.

UNDERSTANDING
GARY SNYDER

CHAPTER ONE

"True Voyage is Return"[*]: Career and Overview

Career

G ary Snyder was born on May 8, 1930, into the poverty of the Depression. A few days before his birth, his out-of-work father, Harold Snyder, landed a job working for a grocery company. A year and a half later, the family moved to the state of Washington, and attempted to make a go of farming. They were generally poorer than their neighbors, with Snyder's father out of work for six or seven years. And when they first moved to Washington, they "lived in a house that was covered with tar paper."[1] Snyder learned to work early in life. By his own account, he did not feel deprived by the lack of money and material goods. His mother, Lois Wilkie Snyder, who aspired to be a writer, introduced him to literature at an early age, and they went frequently to the public library. Snyder became attached to literature and to the physical world around him. "I developed," he says, "a certain amount of self-discipline and an enjoyment in doing a certain amount of work, and then a great attachment to nature."[2] As he explained it to Nicholas O'Connell in 1986: "I grew up . . . in

---

*Ursula K. Le Guin, *The Dispossessed* (New York: Avon, 1975) 68.

close contact with the fabric of nature, rather than removed from it. . . . Growing up in that fabric gave me a powerful moral perspective of respect and regard for all sentient beings and gave me a powerful sense of membership in a real world."[3]

Snyder's family moved to Portland in 1942, and when Snyder was about fifteen his parents separated, with Gary and his younger sister Anthea staying with his mother. Despite moving to the city, Snyder maintained his interest in the outdoors, heavily involved in the study of Native Americans and their ways of life. He spent a few summers working at a YMCA camp on Spirit Lake at the foot of Mount St. Helens and became committed to the experiences of camping, backpacking, and climbing mountains in an alpine wilderness.[4] While attending high school in Portland, he joined an adult mountaineering club, the Mazamas, and the Wilderness Society. At the same time he obtained a part-time job as a copyboy with the *Oregonian* newspaper, where his mother also worked, and began to write poetry because, as he recalls it, "I couldn't find any other way to express what I was feeling about mountaineering on the great snowpeaks of the Northwest."[5] During these years Snyder began living on his own.

In 1947 he enrolled in Reed College, Portland, on a scholarship, and in the summer of 1948, with the help of a friend's father, he sailed from New York on an ocean-going ship working in the steward's department. This experience turned out to be both the start of an engagement with seamanship that lasted into the 1960s and the source of trouble with the government during the McCarthy years of the Cold War. In 1949 he learned an important lesson on wilderness and mountains not from physical immersion but from a poetic perspective. That year he first came across Chinese poetry in translation, which left a deep impression on him. Those poems, he remarked, "freed me from excessive attachment to wild mountains, with their almost subliminal way of presenting even the wildest hills as a place where people, also, live."[6] In the summer of 1950 he worked for the Park Service excavating the archaeological site of Old Fort Vancouver and the following year was employed at a logging camp on the Warm Springs Indian Reservation in Oregon.

For most of the first twenty-one years of his life, then, he shuttled among the rural and urban, lowland and highland areas of the Pacific Northwest. He learned a series of jobs and gained experiences in the wilderness and mountains that would provide ample material for a poetry integrating the routines of physical work with the life of the mind.

Reed College was a tremendously stimulating experience for Snyder and crucial in shaping the intellectual direction of his life. He was influenced not only by some of the teachers he had but also by the community of students, many of whom were aspiring writers. He lived in a large student rental house at 1414 Lambert Street, sharing the basement with Philip Whalen. This house became the source of several lifelong friendships for Snyder.[7] During the summer of his senior year he was briefly married to a college companion, Alison Gass, who shared his interests in hiking and camping. In 1951 he graduated with an interdepartmental degree in anthropology and literature. He wrote an extremely sophisticated undergraduate thesis that was eventually published unrevised as *He Who Hunted Birds in His Father's Village* (1979). By the time he had graduated from college, Snyder had developed as a truly working class intellectual. He had also embarked on his continuing practice of Buddhist *zazen* (sitting meditation).

Poetry had become a passion for him, and he was involved in a group affiliated with the Reed College student arts magazine, *Janus*. Many of these people from Reed remained lifelong friends, such as Philip Whalen and Lew Welch. And while Welch became heavily influenced by William Carlos Williams, who visited Reed, Snyder looked more to Ezra Pound on the one hand and D. H. Lawrence and Robinson Jeffers on the other for poetic guidance.

He was also influenced by Robert Graves's recently published *The White Goddess*. But the decision to become a poet was not made simply or immediately. Initially, he enrolled in graduate school at Indiana University, anticipating earning a Ph.D. But the academic life palled quickly. And after a semester he decided to set himself "loose in the world to sink or swim as a poet."[8] But even though he had made this commitment, it would be a few more years before he clarified his own poetic voice. And that clarity would come from immersion once again in wilderness, specifically the Yosemite California high country in 1955.[9]

In the summer of 1952, back on the West Coast, Snyder went to work as a lookout on Crater Mountain for the U.S. Forestry Service in the Baker National Forest, and the following summer he returned as a lookout on Sourdough Mountain. In the winter months, he lived in San Francisco, part of the time with Whalen, and studied Chinese and Japanese. He was seriously thinking about studying Zen in Japan. He also felt a strong affinity for China, in part as a result of an experience he had as a child. He recounts that somewhere between the ages of nine and eleven, he went into the Seattle Art museum and saw a room full of Chinese landscape paintings. At that moment he felt a deep shock of recognition because they looked to him exactly like the Cascades, the Washington mountains with which he was already familiar. He felt that "the Chinese had an eye for the world that I saw as real."[10]

As a youth Snyder had gravitated toward Native American cultures in his search for an alternative to Judeo-Christian Western culture—including its most recent manifestation, American capitalism—because it seemed the cause of so much suffering in the world. But he realized that such study was not accessible to a white person. One can't study the Hopi way unless one is Hopi, Snyder would remark years later, because that religious practice is limited to tribal members. Mahayana Buddhism, however, is open to anyone who seeks to learn its ways and follow its path. So

Snyder worked on his Japanese and Chinese, taking courses at the University of California at Berkeley, and dreamed of Japan for three years before actually being able to get there.

In 1954, life became complicated. He was blacklisted from the Forest Service and worked in Oregon for a logging company. The following summer he was able to work on a trail crew in the high country of Yosemite National Park. Eventually, Snyder learned that he had been branded a subversive by two different governmental agencies. One was the U.S. Coast Guard, which did so because he had gotten his seaman's card back in 1948 through the assistance of a communist-affiliated maritime union. The other was the F.B.I., which considered some of Snyder's teachers and friends at Reed College members or supporters of the Communist Party. Through a series of letters, queries, and negotiations, including the writing of a loyalty statement of sorts, Snyder eventually cleared his record, which enabled him to obtain a passport.

His letter to the State Department is an interesting document.[11] While Snyder disavows any affiliations with communism, he does admit to having considered himself "an intellectual Marxist" at nineteen—a self-definition he soon dropped in favor of "anarcho-pacifist." He also stands by the statement attributed to him that he "would rather go to a concentration camp than be drafted" into the Korean War. He states unequivocally in his letter that "this is a perfectly legitimate expression of opinion, and one which I still support." And, while pledging not to speak out against the U.S. government while abroad or to incite people against U.S. foreign policy, he also distances himself from any political loyalties. In opposition to large, centralized modern nation states, which he sees as recent arbitrary distinctions imposed on natural societies and nature, Snyder supports decentralized bioregional social organizations. These would be communities based on more ancient models of traditional societies, with territories defined by the lines of the natural boundaries and regions of a particular place. If the

Pacific Northwest were organized bioregionally, parts of Canada and the United States would be joined together and distinct from other parts of those two nations.

The year 1955 was really the pivotal one for Snyder. He worked out his problems with the government, found himself writing a new kind of poetry while in Yosemite, and participated in the famous October 13th Six Gallery reading in San Francisco. At that reading Allen Ginsberg first performed *Howl,* the best-known poem of the 1950s, and Snyder read "A Berry Feast." Snyder had not only found his own voice and cleared the way to pursue his journey to the Far East, but he also established himself as one of the rising young stars of the San Francisco Renaissance. Snyder views himself as part of this renaissance but strongly dissents from any identification with the Beat Movement, which many define as originating on the East rather than the West Coast. Despite their differences, the innovative poets of East and West were often published together and viewed by the public as a single movement. From 1955 onward Snyder's poems tended to be published alongside those of Whalen, Ginsberg, Ferlinghetti, Kerouac, Corso, Rexroth, Duncan, and other "Beat" figures in various poetry magazines internationally and coast to coast. This perception of Snyder as a Beat was further codified in the public consciousness by Jack Kerouac's idealization of him as Japhy Ryder in *The Dharma Bums* (1958). Even though Snyder has repeatedly stated that Kerouac's novel is a work of fiction and strongly objects to people drawing biographical conclusions from it, many still erroneously equate Ryder with Snyder.

In May of 1956, Snyder left San Francisco for Japan, and studied and worked there at a Buddhist temple in conjunction with the activities of the First Zen Institute of America's Kyoto facility, directed by Ruth Sasaki.[12] He had left behind with Robert Creeley the manuscript of *Myths & Texts,* but it would pass through many hands and be rejected by several editors before its publication in 1960. Although it was published a year after *Riprap* (1959), it was completed and organized as a book before many of the poems in that collection were written. Despite the seriousness with which he was approaching Buddhist study, Snyder wrote to a close friend, Will Petersen, in September, 1956: "have come to realize that I am first most a poet. . . . So I don't think I'll ever commit myself to the role of Zen Monk, as free as that role seems to be, because it calls for too much sense of serious responsible behaviour, & no faith in letting poems & such flow out free to everybody."[13] Even after writing this, however, Snyder did have his head shaved, took the Bodhissatva precepts, and studied in and out of monasteries with Buddhist teachers for over ten years in Japan. Once he entered formal koan training with a Zen master, Snyder spent four to five hours a day in formal meditation and had interviews on the koans he was given. (The koan is a theme for meditation. One of the best known and often the first one given students is "What is the sound of one hand clapping?")

Eighteen months later, wanting some time to reflect on Zen and Japan, Snyder took a job as a wiper in the engine room of an oil tanker, the *Sappa Creek,* bound for the Persian Gulf from Yokohama.[14] For eight months he worked at that job as the ship wound its way back and forth to the Persian Gulf, stopping in Italy, Turkey, Okinawa, Ceylon, and various Pacific Islands.

He finally landed in California in April, 1958, and spent nine months in the Bay Area, heavily involved in the poetry scene. The next year *Riprap* was published as his first book by Cid Corman in Japan and distributed in the United States. During this period he met Joanne Kyger. A year later, after something of a whirlwind relationship in San Francisco and a period of vacillation while she was there and Snyder in Japan, Kyger agreed to travel to Kyoto to live with and marry Snyder. It was her first marriage, and Snyder's first real one, and it lasted a stormy, intense four years.[15] The year of his marriage also witnessed the publication by LeRoi Jones of *Myths & Texts.* And, for Snyder, back in Japan, there came a moment of enlightenment.[16]

The entire time he and Kyger were together, with the exception of their six-month sojourn to India in late 1961 and early 1962 (about which Snyder writes in *Passage Through India* [1983]), Snyder studied Buddhism under Oda Sesso Roshi, Rinzai Zen master and Head Abbot of Daitoku-ji Temple, Kyoto. In February, 1964, Kyger returned alone to San Francisco (the years with Snyder are recorded in her book, *The Japan and India Journals 1960-1964* [1981]). By the time Snyder arrived in the Bay Area that fall, the possibility of reconciliation seemed distant and the two resolved to divorce. Snyder taught creative writing at Berkeley and then returned to Japan in October, 1965. That year *Riprap* was republished with the addition of the Han-shan translations, first published in *Evergreen Review* in 1958. The first six sections of *Mountains and Rivers without End,* a long sequence on which Snyder is still working, also appeared in 1965.

The following year Snyder's roshi (his formal Zen master-teacher) died in Kyoto, and Snyder returned briefly to the United States, in time to help preside, with Ginsberg, over the Great Human Be-In in Golden Gate Park in early 1967. When he returned shortly after that to Japan, he turned more outward from the Buddhist community to the Japanese equivalent of the Beat or hippy community, making connections with Nanao Sakaki, a World War II veteran and wandering poet who was organizing communes in Japan. Snyder was also introduced to a graduate student in English literature, Masa Uehara, and they married in 1967 on the lip of an active volcano on Suwa-no-se Island in the Toshima archipelago, south of Kyushu. The two of them were living there with Sakaki and a dozen or so others in a subsistence communal experiment. The poems of the first three sections of *Regarding Wave* (1969) come from this period of 1967 and 1968, when Gary and Masa were first married and she gave birth to their first son, Kai, in Japan. Shortly after Kai's birth, the Snyders returned permanently to the United States, with Snyder looking forward to participating in what he perceived as the rise of the ecology movement. The next year, 1969, their second son, Gen, was born. During this period Snyder was busy publishing books with New Directions—*The Back Country* (1968), *Earth House Hold* (1969), and then *Regarding Wave* (1970), as well as publishing collections in England. He received various awards and increasing recognition in the United States for his poetry. Not until he received the Pulitzer Prize for Poetry in 1975 would he receive as many accolades as during his final years in Japan.

What accounted for such attention? Dan McLeod argues that it was far more than Snyder's poetry: "the example of Snyder's life and values offered a constructive, albeit underground, alternative to mainstream American culture." He goes on to claim that "Snyder's main impact on the Beat Generation, and on American literature since, has been as a spokesperson for the natural world and the values associated with primitive cultures. But his poetic use of Asian sources has also been influential."[17]

After his return to California, Snyder's influence spread further, beyond literary circles increasingly to environmental and American Buddhist circles. His 1970 Earth Day speech at Colorado State College and the following year's talk at the Center for the Study of Democratic Institutions, Santa Barbara, formed part of a growing practice of lecturing on environmental and international issues. During this time, with the help of others, he built his home outside of Nevada City on the edge of the Tahoe National Forest and named it Kitkitdizze, "the Indian word for a local plant called Mountain Misery."[18] In 1972 he participated in the United Nations Conference on Human Environment in Stockholm. Such lecturing and conference participation led to his writing an increasing amount of prose, as evidenced by *Earth House Hold, The Old Ways* (1977), and most recently *The Practice of the Wild* (1990), with other talks and essays as yet uncollected.

Poetry has never been left behind. In 1973 he published *The Fudo Trilogy,* a limited-edition collection that includes "Smokey the Bear Sutra." The next year *Turtle Island,* his most politically engaged volume, was published by New Directions and won him the 1975 Pulitzer. Snyder defines this volume as ''the first literary surfacing of the bioregional concept.''[19] He was heavily involved during these years in the California Arts Council and ecological work, both locally and internationally. And from such involvement came *Axe Handles* (1983), a collection with a very different tone, less apocalyptic, and less confrontational than *Turtle Island.* As the shift from *The Back Country* to *Regarding Wave* displays a transformation from doubt, struggle, difficulty, to rapture and attainment, so too the transformation between the two later volumes, *Turtle Island* and *Axe Handles,* may be said to move from an immediacy and confrontation of political struggle to a long-range, evolutionary process of cultural change.

Age may very well have been a factor in Snyder's change of emphasis; also, the growth of his children and the promise of another generation to carry on the lessons already learned may have enabled him to feel less anxious about the future. Snyder commented on this change during an interview in 1983: ''If *Turtle Island* was a statement about what life in North America could be . . . *Axe Handles* is a much more low-key presentation of what the moves are when you really make a place your home.''[20] There may be something of a retrospective involved as well. That same year, 1983, *Passage Through India,* the journal of his trip in the early 1960s with Kyger, was published in book form. And in 1986 *Left Out in the Rain: New Poems 1947-1985* appeared, pulling together some 150 previously uncollected poems from his high school days to the present.

Through it all, Snyder continues to promise completion of *Mountains and Rivers without End.* But his most recent book, as well as the one projected beyond it, is prose. The essay collection *The Practice of the Wild* (1990) develops Snyder's major ecological ideas, particularly his perception of planetary thinking and bioregional consciousness, to their most fully articulated conception. These he developed in part through using drafts of the essays in courses he taught at the University of California, Davis, where he has been a professor since 1985. Snyder's life has taken an additional new turn beyond his appointment in academia and his being named a member of the American Academy and Institute of Arts and Letters. He and Masa divorced in 1987. Snyder has since married Carole Koda, a third-generation Japanese American with two daughters.

In a recent interview Snyder characterized his current artistic practice: "I see my role as trying to present some alternatives, and to tell people what the normal world was or could be like if we took on the job of reknitting our connections with each other and with the natural world. The fact is that the modern human condition in the last 60 or 70 years has gone against the norm of the last 40,000 years, and we don't know yet what it means."[21] This emphasis on teaching and "telling" complements Snyder's emphasis within poetry on orality and performance. The Beats revitalized the notion of poetry as performance and Snyder shares with them a lifelong commitment to the poetry reading as a cultural practice. He remarked in 1984 on the resurgence of storytelling in the United States: "it has to do, in part, with poetry reading and the efforts of poets for the last 15 or 20 years to re-validate oral literature. . . . And that poetry in particular has its true manifestation in the act of performance and, indeed, all literary experience has its truest manifestation in the oral mode."[22] These words address the immediate moment, what one might call the "Now" of poetry practice, the lyric intensity and presentness. In the same interview Snyder also addressed the other side of poetry, the mythographic, the perpetual, the evolutionary: "The deepest and most profound work is that of transforming the fundamental archetype by which this culture has operated for the last four or five thousand years. . . . And what's really interesting to my mind is the 'political' work of poetry on the fundamental myth-archetypes, transforming the very way we see the world."[23]

Overview

The preceding pages set out the highlights of Snyder's career by means of a chronology of events. In this section, the major features of Snyder's intellectual and spiritual development will be outlined. Snyder frequently resorts to the Buddhist imagery of Indra's jeweled net to depict the interconnectedness of all existence. While the individual trajectory of a single physical life may be laid out linearly, the life of the mind does not conform to such a structure. A more appropriate image for intellectual growth is that of the net, which has threads, but threads that radiate out from one another, forming eventually a circle, a curved universe.

So too Snyder's concerns loop back and circle out from identification with the "ghosts of trees," whom he feels were teaching him in his youth in Washington, to learning to write "about a pine tree as a pine tree would want to be written about, from inside," to becoming a biosphere spokesperson: "part of my life project has been proposing the possibility of speaking from the nonhuman to the human, because the human does not hear enough from the nonhuman."[24] Such a role can be seen in Snyder's activism in the Buddhist Peace Fellowship founded in 1977. Speaking about its purpose before a benefit poetry reading in 1985, Snyder stated that "it's part of our mission—as we've defined it—as Buddhists to extend the concern for peace outside the human realm to the nonhuman realm; . . . issues of peace which affect us now in the world affect all of us, including plants and animals and watersheds, lakes and rivers, mountains and glaciers."[25]

What makes Snyder's poetry difficult for many readers is not any single aspect of it. True, in some poems he is highly allusive, referring to Japanese folklore, Hindu mythology, or Buddhist philosophical tenets and terms not known by the average American reader. All of this, of course, makes it difficult to capture the full range of meaning playing through a single poem, and particularly through his two sequences, *Myths & Texts* and *Mountains and Riv-*

ers without End. But sometimes, his very simple, brief lyric poems seem just as difficult because Snyder draws on such a range of
knowledge and experience. He has so synthesized and integrated
diverse cultural materials that the context in which the poem is
written and the context most suitable for its reading are often not
evident.

Snyder does frequently point to, name, and suggest new areas
for study for the reader. He also puts material together in unfa-
miliar ways, altering or questioning common points of view and
traditional perceptions of relationships in order to get his reader
to rethink American culture's most basic assumptions and
presumptions.

Three areas comprise the heart of Snyder's resources for his poetry. The first consists of the cultures of inhabitory or primitive
peoples, particularly the Native American tribes of the Pacific
West. Other primal people who have influenced him are the Ainu
of Japan, the Hawaiians, the Alaskan Eskimos, and the Australian
aborigines. The specific and practical relationships of these peoples' cultures to the land, to the place where they practice their
existence, are crucial for Snyder. He believes that these peoples
have much to teach urban societies about regaining a balanced,
sustaining relationship between human culture and the natural
environment. Before Snyder knew anything about Buddhism, he
was learning about Native Americans, and he renewed that study
and contact when he returned to the United States at the end of
the 1960s.[26]

The second area consists of the Asian cultures of China, Japan,
and, to a lesser extent, India and Tibet, particularly in terms of
their Buddhist practices and life-styles, and Buddhism's religious
precursors in these countries. Snyder identifies himself as a Zen
Buddhist, because that is the discipline he has studied and in which
he was immersed for many of his years in Japan. But even within
Zen he showed an eclectic and interdisciplinary tendency through
his contact not just with the Rinzai sect of his own temple but also

with Soto, Yamabushi, Jodo, and Kegon. His explanation of the Zen practice at the Ring of Bone Zendo near his home gives some sense of this syncretic spirit: "It was not so much Zen as it was Chan. By that I mean not so narrowly monastic and Japanese, but more 'Chinese'—earlier, less codified, more ecumenical, ecological, and playful. . . . creative commitments to a women-men-babies-house-soil-and-All Beings—being together spirit has been central to the inspiration of this Sangha for years."[27]

The third area consists of ecology, a concern of Snyder's throughout his life. Clearly, when he was very young, Snyder intuited a harmonious relationship with nature and sensed that American culture was violating that harmony. As the years went by his sense of ecological criteria for evaluating philosophies, beliefs, and practices deepened. His permanent return to the United States after the period of spiritual growth in Japan largely coincided with the recognition of ecology not simply as a legitimate science but as a long-term movement for major, evolutionary and revolutionary cultural change. In the Earth Day speech he gave at Colorado State College, Greeley, on April 22, 1970, he stated unequivocally that "the moment I stepped foot on this soil after having been away that long [almost fifteen years], I immediately got into the ecological battle—the only battle that counts now, the only thing that matters to me anymore."[28] And twenty years later, in another Earth Day speech, he looked back at that moment: "That day was not exactly a beginning, but it was a hinge, a moment of transformation. It marked the gradual closing of the Viet-Nam War and anti-war activism, and the turning of that energy toward another war, the war against earth."[29]

Snyder's remark that ecology was the only thing that mattered has never meant that primitive peoples have ceased to be a concern and source of inspiration and education or that he is no longer practicing Zen. He does so on a daily basis, both in terms of meditation and in terms of Buddhist activism. Ecology, as signaled by the title of his first prose volume, *Earth House Hold*—which is a pun on the Greek root for the word *ecology*—is the social and political focus for what he has learned. For Snyder to be a Buddhist and not an ecologist would be a travesty; and to be an ecologist means that a person, consciously or not, is living a life that shares practices found in Buddhism and primitive cultures. He also remarked in his 1970 Earth Day speech that "the people who are beginning to understand how these networks and relationships function are the ones who can also comprehend that ancient, primitive, archaic religious world view which is the true ethic, the biological ethic, morality that includes all beings."

The whole spinning universe, humans included, is interconnected, interdependent, and interanimating for Snyder, and he would have his readers see that too. All of it is living and being, although in states and conditions that may not appear to be so according to contemporary perceptions and definitions of life. The idea of the earth as a living organism consisting of equally living parts is a concept that informs all three of Snyder's major areas of concern: the traditions of primitive peoples, Buddhist thought, and the science of ecology. He represents the earth as organism through his frequent depictions of it as mother, as goddess, and, specifically, as Gaia.

The underlying philosophical assumptions and cultural beliefs, the themes, allusions, and symbols are not the only sources of difficulty for some readers of Snyder's poetry. Form may also prove difficult, but only at first. Two major sources for Snyder's poetics need to be recognized. One is the free verse of Anglo-American modernism as practiced by such poets as T. S. Eliot, Ezra Pound, William Carlos Williams, and Marianne Moore. In particular, Snyder's form involves a specific development in free verse known as field composition, in which the entire page provides a canvas for the laying out of the lines of the poem. E. E. Cummings is probably the American poet most widely known for field composition, but it was most developed as a poetics by the Beats and the Black Mountain poets, led by Charles Olson, who influenced Snyder. In

Snyder's *Myths & Texts* and *Regarding Wave* the application of field composition is evident in poem after poem. In other volumes it is less pronounced.

For Snyder, free verse and field composition open up the poetic form to flexibility and variation. These in turn enable the presentation of differing perceptions of relationships between words, between language and thought, and between words and things: "Each poem grows from an energy-mind-field-dance, and has its own inner grain."[30] Snyder sees written poetry as arising from and continuing to be based on oral performance. Field composition, then, is a way of "scoring" the poem, as in musical composition, for the way in which it ought to be performed when read or sung aloud. When Snyder uses the word *song* in a poem title he is using it literally rather than figuratively.[31]

Another source of significant formal influence on Snyder has been classical Chinese and Japanese poetics. Some of Snyder's first translation work at Berkeley involved translating the Chinese poems of Han-shan into English, which he later reworked in Japan. These exercises are the "Cold Mountain Poems," added to the volume *Riprap* when it was reprinted in 1965. The specific characteristics of the Chinese and Japanese languages, both of which Snyder knows, contribute to the differences between these poetics and that of the Anglo-American tradition. Spoken Chinese is a relatively monosyllabic, word-order language, using tones phonemically (the same sound with a different tone represents an entirely different word in Chinese, unlike in English). It is also what one might call a "word-order" language in that the order in which the words appear structures the meaning in a way that does not occur in English. Written Chinese intensifies these characteristics, because it relies on ideograms (characters) rather than on words and letters. Chinese, then, expresses poetic images in blocks and concise phrases, often without verbs and with no equivalents of English-language prepositions and articles. And classical Chinese, the language of much of the Asian poetry Snyder studies, is tenseless.[32]

Likewise, the Japanese language has a very different syntax and grammar than English. Unlike Chinese, it is not phonemic and is polysyllabic; but like Chinese, Japanese is not inflected. Neither language can have the kind of metrical verse that dominated English-language poetry into the twentieth century. Snyder eschews metrics, and in his poems the frequent absence of articles stands out. He also often uses infinitives and participles, *to go* and *going,* rather than subject + verb constructions in his poems, so that actions occur but no "I" claims control. The poems of *Riprap* are replete with such practices, reflecting Asian poetic influences. As a result the speaker of a Snyder poem often remains unidentified, or a poem may contain no complete sentences, or the temporal relationships of cause and effect may remain unstated.

Another evidence of Asian influence in Snyder's work is that thematic or emotive points are often made, as they are in Chinese, by means of the juxtaposition of two images rather than through metaphor or simile. As Laszlo Géfin notes, "in its unadorned, unpretentious simplicity and quick juxtapositions of natural data, the Snyder poem comes closest perhaps to the Fenollosian definition of the Chinese ideogram: 'a vivid shorthand picture of the operations of nature.' "[33] Pound learned this technique from Chinese poetry and encouraged its use in modernist works, but Snyder learned it more from the source than from Pound. Finally, from the Japanese haiku form, as well as the classical Chinese poems he studied, Snyder learned to write poems that have no stated moral or no authorial observation. As in haiku (a very short and concise three-line Japanese verse form), Snyder often depicts the thing in itself, in its moment of being rather than in its serving a metaphorical purpose for the intellectualizing mind or individual emotions. People are frequently not the center of Snyder's attention, as they are in much Romantic poetry, nor are they the reason for the existence or behavior of other beings.

Snyder's strange-looking poems may take the reader trained on sonnets, iambic pentameter, and rhyming couplets some time to get used to. But the easiest way to adjust to the rhythms and structures of one of these poems is to read it aloud, using the line breaks and the blank spaces as cues for when to pause and how long, and when to emphasize certain words. Another way to get a feel for Snyder's poetics is to read some collections of traditional Japanese and classical Chinese poems in translation, such as haiku by Bashō.

Many of Snyder's poems require of the reader no special preparation to be enjoyed and appreciated, whether or not all of the nuances are noticed, allusions registered, and styles recognized. Much of the learning that the more complex poems demands is provided at least in outline in Snyder's many essays and interviews. And the continually increasing amount of Snyder criticism is making much of the seemingly exotic and arcane more accessible. But the main point that needs to be made is that the work is worth it, because the poetry poses and offers solutions to some of the most critical questions facing American culture today. Snyder is a visionary poet as well as a political one. He offers possibilities and potentialities for humanity's future in relationship with nature, as well as criticizing and analyzing the errors of present and past ways. Snyder and such other contemporary writers as Susan Griffin, John Haines, Joy Harjo, Ursula K. Le Guin, Barry Lopez, Mary Oliver, Leslie Marmon Silko, and Alice Walker are working to help shape a new cultural paradigm, one that they hope will build a culture based on healing rather than ravaging the rest of nature.

Notes

1. See Nicholas O'Connell, *At The Field's End* (Seattle: Madrona Publishers, 1987) 309. The figures here are based on Snyder's emendation of his remarks to O'Connell.

2. Snyder quoted by David Kherdian, "Gary Snyder," in *Six Poets of the San Francisco Renaissance: Portraits and Checklists* (Fresno, Ca.: Giligia Press, 1967) 47.

3. O'Connell 309.

4. See Jerry Crandall's reminiscences, "Mountaineers Are Always Free," in *Gary Snyder: Dimensions of a Life,* ed. Jon Halper (San Francisco: Sierra Club Books, 1991) 3–7.

5. O'Connell 312.

6. Snyder quoted by Dan McLeod, "Gary Snyder," in *The Beats: Literary Bohemians in Postwar America, Part 2, Dictionary of Literary Biography,* vol. 16, ed. Ann Charters (Detroit: Gale, 1983) 495. See also Crandall 6.

7. See the following: J. Michael Mahar, "Scenes from the Sidelines," and Carol Baker, "1414 SE Lambert Street," in Halper 8–15 and 24–29.

8. Snyder quoted by Kherdian 49.

9. For details on this experience, see David Robertson, "Gary Snyder Rip-rapping in Yosemite, 1955," *American Poetry* 2.1 (1984) 52–59.

10. Snyder has recounted this story several times. See Barry Chowka, "The East West Interview," in *Gary Snyder: The Real Work, Interviews & Talks, 1964–1979,* ed. Wm. Scott McLean (New York: New Directions, 1980) 94; McLeod 189; and O'Connell 313–14.

11. The correspondence between Snyder and the Departments of the Interior and State, as well as his notarized sworn statement of 18 March 1955, are in the Gary Snyder Archives, Department of Special Collections, University of California Library, Davis.

12. On this period in Snyder's life, see Burton Watson, "Kyoto in the Fifties"; Philip Yampolsky, "Kyoto, Zen, Snyder"; and Hisao Kanaseki, "An Easy Rider at Yase," in Halper 53–59; 60–69; and 70–75.

13. Letter to Will Petersen, 17 September 1956, published in *Io* no. 14 (Summer 1972) 80.

14. See Snyder's letter to Lew Welch, 14 September 1957, published in *I Remain: The Letters of Lew Welch & The Correspondence of His Friends,* 2 vols., ed. Donald Allen (Bolinas, Ca.: Grey Fox Press, 1980), vol. 1, 112–14.

15. See Yampolsky 66 and Kanaseki 73.

16. See Katsunori Yamazato, "Seeking a Fulcrum: Gary Snyder and Japan (1956–1975)," Ph. D. dissertation, University of California, Davis, 1987, 89–90.

17. McLeod 487–88.

18. Burr Snider, "The Sage of the Sierra," *Image: San Francisco Examiner* 17 Sept. 1989: 10; see also Yamazato 114–17, 128–29.

19. O'Connell 318.

20. Michael Helm, "A Conversation with Gary Snyder," *California Living Magazine, Sunday San Francisco Examiner & Chronicle* 20 November 1983: 17.

21. Snider 16.

22. Luke Breit and Pat Grizzell, "The Recovery of the Commons: Interview with Gary Snyder and Steve Sanfield," *Poet News* (May 1984) 1; see O'Connell 319.

23. Breit and Grizzell 10.

24. O'Connell 320.

25. Uri Hertz, "An Interview with Gary Snyder," *Third Rail* 7 (1985–86) 52.

26. Bruce Cook, *The Beat Generation* (New York: Scribner's, 1971) 33. See also Michael Castro, *Interpreting the Indian: Twentieth-Century Poets and the American Indian* (Albuquerque: University of New Mexico Press, 1984).

27. Quoted in Yamazato 129; from Gary Snyder, "A Brief Account of the Ring of Bone Zendo, I," *Ring of Bone Zendo Newsletter* (15 October 1986) 8–9.

28. "Earth Day Speech," April 22, 1970, Colorado State College. Unpublished. Photocopy in Gary Snyder Archives, Department of Special Collections, University of California Library, Davis. Quoted by permission of Gary Snyder.

29. "Earth Day and the War Against the Imagination." Speech "for Earth Day April 22, 1990, at Bridgeport on the South Yuba River in Nevada County / Nisenan Country / Western Slopes / Northern Sierra / Shasta Bioregion / Continent of Turtle Island." Unpublished. Quoted by permission of Gary Snyder.

30. Quoted in Bob Steuding, *Gary Snyder* (Boston: Twayne, 1976) 35.

31. Lee Bartlett, "Interview: Gary Snyder," *California Quarterly* No. 9 (1975) 47.

32. See Jody Norton, "The Importance of Nothing: Absence and Its Origins in the Poetry of Gary Snyder," *Contemporary Literature* 28 (1987) 44–47, rpt. in *Critical Essays on Gary Snyder,* ed. Patrick D. Murphy (Boston: G. K. Hall, 1990) 166-88; Yao-fu Lin, " 'The Mountains are Your Mind': Orientalism in the Poetry of Gary Snyder," *Tamkang Review* 6–7 (1975–1976) 366–67; Wai-Lim Yip, "Classical Chinese and Modern Anglo-American Poetry: Convergence of Language and Poetry," *Comparative Literature Studies* 11 (1974) 21–47; also, Ling Chung, "Whose Mountain Is This?—Gary Snyder's Translation of Han Shan," *Renditions* 7 (Spring 1977) 93–102.

33. Laszlo Géfin, *Ideogram: History of a Poetic Method* (Austin: University of Texas Press, 1982) 130. The section of this book treating Snyder is reprinted as "[Ellipsis and Riprap: Gary Snyder]" in Murphy 122-31.

CHAPTER TWO

From Myth Criticism to Mythopoeia: *Myths & Texts*

In the early 1950s Snyder produced two full-length works, one critical and one poetic, *He Who Hunted Birds in His Father's Village* (1979) and *Myths & Texts* (1960). The former is his undergraduate thesis written in 1951. While it is of interest in its own right as an anthropological study of a particular Native American myth, it is more important as a document informing the directions and concerns of Snyder's poetry. As he says in the foreword to the published version, "I went on to other modes of study and writing, but never forgot what I learned from this work."[1] And Nathaniel Tarn, in the preface, claims that "the basic themes of Snyder's work, many of which appear in filigree in the thesis, are all set out in *Myths & Texts*"(p. xvi). This connection is not surprising given that Snyder started writing the poems for this sequence within a year of graduation.

He Who Hunted is Snyder at work as myth critic, the career he initially envisioned for himself and which took him to graduate school in anthropology. But he turned abruptly from that path and became a myth handler instead. In much of his poetry, but nowhere more fully embodied than *Myths & Texts,* Snyder practices mythopoeia, the adaptive retelling and creating of myths that have guided or are needed to guide a culture.

21

Myths & Texts also shows Snyder working toward his own voice as a poet but in some ways not yet finding the form to embody that voice in poetic structures. He believes himself that not until three-fourths of the way through the period in which he wrote the sequence did he find a way of writing poetry that was original rather than derivative. This development of voice can be discerned through a comparison of *Myths & Texts* with *Riprap*. The latter collection is the one that most critics start with when analyzing Snyder's career, as Tim Dean does in *Gary Snyder and the American Unconscious*.[2] But starting with *Riprap*, simply because it was published a year before the other book, creates confusion, as when Dean attempts to compare it with the first edition of Whitman's *Leaves of Grass*.[3] Some critics see Snyder's style floundering, turning back toward modernism rather than forward to something more innovative because they fail to realize that *Myths & Texts* was nearly finished before the *Riprap* poems were started.[4]

As various critics have noted, *Myths & Texts* is far more indebted to Pound and Eliot than to Asian influences. As a result, the references to Hinduism and Buddhism are based primarily on reading rather than experience, and Japanese allusions are rare.[5] The structure strongly echoes the kind of juxtaposition that one finds in Eliot's *The Waste Land* and Pound's *Cantos*. But the ideas are Snyder's and, unlike any of the modernist works it emulates structurally, those ideas are informed by a wealth of Native American myths and practices.

A look at Snyder's undergraduate honors thesis, then, provides some clues for understanding *Myths & Texts*. In *He Who Hunted*, Snyder states: ''Original mind speaks through little myths and tales that tell us how to *be* in some specific ecosystem of the far-flung world'' (p. x). Snyder surmises: ''Myth is a 'reality lived' because for every individual it contains, at the moment of telling, the projected content of both his unarticulated and conscious values: simultaneously ordering, organizing, and making comprehensible the world within which the values exist. One might even reformulate the statement to say 'Reality is a myth lived' '' (109-10).

Myth, then, places people in a cultural and physical matrix, providing them with a coherent sense of presence in place and time. Snyder also defines the role of the poet in modern society, tying it into this conception of myth: ''the poet would not only be creating private mythologies for his readers, but moving toward the formation of a new social mythology'' (112). As Snyder understands it, the poet acts as vehicle for a social mythology that seeks to reintegrate individual, society, and ecosystem.

He thus brings to the creation of *Myths & Texts* a strongly developed sense of the social role of myths, the responsibility of the poet, and the kind of consciousness that myth must help create, integrate, and maintain in the contemporary world. *Myths & Texts* produces an interplay between the two kinds of information linked in the title,''the two sources of human knowledge,'' until at the end they become complementary descriptions of one experience.[6] The ''texts'' consist of sensory experiences undergone by speakers in the poem as well as the previous experiences of historical figures who are either the speakers or subjects of little stories. Similarly, one finds two kinds of ''myths'' in the poem: allusions to and brief stories about primitive and ancient myths of previous cultures; little stories and mythopoeic elements—figures, events, locales—that contribute to ''the formation of a new social mythology,'' a task of the sequence explicitly stated in ''Hunting 1.'' For Snyder, as William J. Jungels notes, ''it is probably generally true that myths serve as much to sustain and encourage a culture in its practices and values as to simply reflect them.''[7] In addition, myths serve as a means for presenting a new spiritual perception of the contemporary world. In this context, then, what may have been or may be at the moment a ''text,'' an external sensory experience, may become through the work of mythopoeia part of a little ''myth'' that will ''tell us how to *be* in some specific ecosystem.''

The first passage of *Myths & Texts,* "Logging 1," opens with "The morning star is not a star." This line functions as a text making a factual statement about the planet Venus, while suggesting that the mind can misinterpret sense impressions. Paraphrasing Thoreau's remark in *Walden* that "the sun is but a morning star," it also functions as a myth element. It alludes to *Walden* not simply as a literary work but as an American myth, because that book has become an element of the romantic image of American individualism and self-reliance. The negation itself, implying false vision, begins the section on an ominous note, one prefigured by the epigraph from Acts 19:27, which refers to Christian attacks on the worship of the goddess Diana. The second and third lines, "Two seedling fir, one died / Io, Io," present another text and then a refrain alluding to one of the manifestations of the Great Mother and a myth with a wandering hero.[8] This refrain also responds to the epigraph by referring to another form of goddess worship. The next two lines describe the initial garbing for a mythic celebration. The quotation "The May Queen / Is the survival of / A pre-human / Rutting season" then produces a textual gloss of the myth. In these few lines "myth" as the religious story about a universal cultural experience and "text" as the record of actual experience are woven together.

The second stanza of "Logging 1" reads:

> The year spins
> Pleiades sing to their rest
>   at San Francisco
>   dream
>   dream
> Green comes out of the ground
> Birds squabble
> Young girls run mad with the pine bough,
>   Io[.] (3)

From Myth Criticism to Mythopoeia

The first line presents a text connecting human conception of time with earth's physical cycles. The next line mixes myth and text: a setting constellation is described by means of its accompanying myth. The reader is given a physical location, but the invocation of "dream / dream" suggests the sensory realm of the collective unconscious, the locus for mythic vision. Then springtime is indicated through descriptions of animal and plant life, and this text is linked to the myth of that season by the following line, which describes, in Howard McCord's words, "the thyrsus, carried by maenads worshipping Dionysus."[9] In some myths, Io is the mother of Dionysus. Turned into a heifer by Hera because Zeus lusted after her, Io was forced to wander for years before regaining human form. Dionysus was also a wanderer, but more importantly he is associated with rituals of the changing seasons. Snyder may be making connections not only between spring and fertility but also between wandering and homecoming. But the physical location of the Pleiades star system indicates the season as autumn, with spring existing only as a dream. Jungels interprets this juxtaposition of seasons in this way: "With the goddesses retired and the earth devastated it is only in dream that spring and Io . . . can be conjured" (17). The autumnal setting suggests that the matrifocal/Earth-worshiping values are waning, which prepares for the transition to the quotation from Exodus 34:13 that opens "Logging 2."

The quotation Snyder chooses historically prefigures the poem's epigraph, Acts 19:27, with both depicting attacks on matrifocal, nature-worship religions. The next line describes ancient China's denuding of its forests and subsequent ground erosion. This juxtaposition links the destructive character of widely divergent "advanced" civilizations, indicating that Snyder recognizes that the anti-ecological drive is not limited to the West but has occurred and continues worldwide. In the following lines the use of "killed" in relation to the forests asserts the living quality of trees and "in their own praise" places the entire description within a religious, mythic framework. In addition to the intertwining of myth and text, Snyder foreshadows the other two sections of the sequence. "Hunting" will address reverent and sacrilegious ways of killing. "Burning" will treat fire as part of nature's cleansing, regenerative cycle of growth and decay. At this point, however, one only has sacrilegious killing and burning without regeneration.

The narrator comments in stanza four: "I wake from bitter dreams," a contrast with the invocation of "dream / dream." Snyder follows this bitter stanza with one that again interweaves myth and text:

> "Pines grasp the clouds with iron claws
> like dragons rising from sleep"
> 250,000 board-feet a day
> If both Cats keep working
> & nobody gets hurt[.] (4)

Although the pines and Cats form part of the experiential text of logging, they also can serve as symbols for the creation of a logging myth. An essential difference exists, though, between the pines-as-dragons myth, with its Chinese fertility symbolism (Jungels 26), and any modern logging myth. The "iron claws" grasp but do not devour the clouds, while the Cats devour the pines as dead "board-feet." "Logging 3" opens with a quotation describing the Lodgepole Pine. In juxtaposition to the preceding mythopoeic quotation, this one is a textbook definition, but one which provides a phoenixlike archetypal symbol: a tree whose new life arises from seedcones gestating in the ashes of the tree-consuming fire. This symbol counters the destructive burning of "Logging 2." The second stanza describes the process of hooking felled trees. Snyder follows this vignette with a tale of the ancient Chinese figure Hsü Fang who lived a life diametrically opposed to the destructive one that demands the rape of forests.[10] A story of modern life follows and concludes with a regenerative remark: "The kids grow up and go to college / They don't come back. / The little fir-trees do."

"Logging 3" ends:

> Rocks the same blue as sky
> Only icefields a mile up,
>
>   are the mountain
> Hovering over ten thousand acres
> Of young fir. (5)

This text of sensory experience contains essential elements for Snyder's mythopoeia. The mountain plays a crucial role in "Burning" as its height provides the physical opportunity for a different perception of the world, paralleling the opportunity for a changed psychological perception that dreaming can provide. Here "Hovering" animates the mountain, reinforcing the image of living earth, and the stanza concludes by reiterating the image of natural regeneration that began it.

The rest of "Logging" continues these patterns. Passages "4" and "5" produce an intermixing of myth and text similar to the first three. Passages "6" and "7" produce stories from the recent past that are already beginning to take on aspects of "little myths," with "6" being "the voice of Snyder's father, taken down without his awareness" (Jungels 32). This passage tells of the natural profundity of second-growth regeneration, the rapid spread of new kinds of trees and bushes on logged-off land, experienced by Snyder's father in his own youth. "Logging 7" tells of the Wobbly (Industrial Workers of the World) days in Washington state and how these experiences have led to slogans that have their own symbolic, and potentially mythic, characteristics. "8" and "9" focus almost exclusively on individual physical experiences, but from "Logging 10" to the end, the mythic elements begin to increase in length in relation to the text elements with the exception of a lull in "13."

In "Logging 13," the narrator describes a natural forest fire and observes it as lookout rather than as logger. He concludes: "The crews have departed, / And I am not concerned." This passage, like the last stanza of "Logging 3," uses description of natural processes to develop reader awareness of a state of mind. The narrator's lack of concern suggests a changing perception of ecological activity. From this psychological vantage point, "Logging 14" looks back through history at all the destruction wrought by various societies, each with its own myths, and brings the survey up to the present of the Puritan-capitalist myth governing America. It also specifically condemns the destruction of Native American societies. This passage closes with an experience rendered as myth, contrasting regenerative fires identified elsewhere with this destructive one:

> Sawmill temples of Jehovah.
> Squat black burners 100 feet high
> Sending the smoke of our burnt
> Live sap and leaf
> To his eager nose. (15)

This stanza serves first as a mythic representation of a text experience; second, as an experiential evaluation of the results of a still-functioning religious myth: Christianity, which continues to guide much of American society.

"Logging" concludes with a passage entirely composed of myth fragments. "Logging 15" proposes a source for society's guiding myths other than the Judeo-Christian tradition. It draws on Hinduism and Buddhism for its perception of the interpenetrating movement of natural life and human social life and culminates by seeking solace in the Hindu teleology of the kalpa cycle.[11] This seeking produces a multiplicity of tonalities, from anger to sorrow and confidence to pessimism, which suggests the conclusion's tentative character. The way of life so far portrayed proves insufficient to cope with the relationship of society and nature. In like manner, the culmination of insights proves insufficient to resolve the contradictions of that relationship.

From Myth Criticism to Mythopoeia

Lodgepole
>cone/seed waits for fire
And then thin forests of silver-gray.
>in the void
>a pine cone falls
Pursued by squirrels
What mad pursuit! What struggle to escape!

Her body a seedpod
Open to the wind
"A seed pod void of seed
We had no meeting together"
>so you and I must wait
Until the next blaze
Of the world, the universe,
Millions of worlds, burning
>—oh let it lie. (16)

In the first half of "15" the Lodgepole Pine stands as a symbol of earth's regenerative cycles, including fiery destruction. The pursuit of the squirrels followed by the line from Keats's "Ode on a Grecian Urn" produces both a lighthearted tone and an emphasis on fertility. The second stanza, though, abruptly reverses the tone, embedding a text of unfulfilled pairing between myth fragments of sterility and cleansing. Snyder intensifies the reversal through the diametrically opposed uses of "void"—one of these being the positive Buddhist sense of it as emptiness and the other the American meaning of sterility. Snyder suggests that hope lies in the mythic cycle of rebirth, rather than in the physical regeneration of the society depicted in "Logging."

The third stanza picks up the apocalyptic image of the kalpa cycle's end initiated in the previous stanza. The first two lines—"Shiva at the end of the kalpa: / Rock-fat, hill-flesh, gone in a whiff''—state the mythic apocalypse of the world's body. The next lines denounce modern society and its Judeo-Christian antecedents. But the narrator pulls himself up short with ''Let them lie.'' He has condemned but not as yet offered an alternative. Further, his own seeking of solace in the cycles beyond humanity's meddling encourages passivity because he does not commit himself to changing the present human condition. The resignation of the second stanza, reiterated by the repetition of ''let them lie,'' deflates the anger of the third.

The opening lines of stanza four present a text of natural activity, but one of mythic proportions. In opposition to the cutting of groves, ''flowers crack the pavement.'' These images return to the mood of the opening stanza. The old Chinese saying, however, that closes the passage—'' 'The brush / may paint the mountains and streams / Though the territory is lost' '' (16)—questions nature's ability to succeed in its regeneration, providing no reassurance that the ''territory'' will not ''be lost.'' The question stands at the end of ''Logging'': can the damage of modern society be undone, or will humanity so damage the system that it must collapse before regenerating? And its corollary, addressed to both poet and reader: can anything be done or must people merely wait, watch, and record the death? The quotation suggests some reassurance in the word ''may'' but provides no promise.

''Hunting'' opens with the ''first shaman song,'' which provides the beginning of a response to ''Logging.'' If ''Logging'' exemplifies by reference to Judeo-Christian capitalism that ''Myth is a 'reality lived,' '' then ''Hunting,'' by means of Snyder's uses of primitivism and shamanism, exemplifies that ''Reality is a myth lived.'' Or, as Jungels puts it, ''Snyder sees hunting, meditation, and shamanism as all part of the same complex of human perception'' (61). ''Hunting 1'' ends with the speaker sitting ''without thoughts'' at the edge of the logging road ''Hatching a new myth'' (19). Snyder uses the participle ''hatching'' with precision. Throughout ''Hunting'' humanity's life will be intimately tied to the life cycles of animals and the myths surrounding them. Jungels has uncovered the old myths behind "Hunting," "those of the coastal Salish" (68). This background of Native American hunting and food-gathering myths, with their attendant shamanistic beliefs, bolsters the narrator in his own hunting and gathering of the mythic material the next culture needs.

"Hunting 3" and "Hunting 4" focus on birds. In "3" Snyder defines the text of living birds, then describes their role in divination and links that religious role with writing: "Form: dots in air changing from line to line" (20). The narrator is connected with the seer or shaman in the role of preserving the myths of animals. The last line also suggests that not only do myths define the future through ritual but also that the birds, as a synecdoche for all of nature, determine humanity's future.

The second stanza begins with a description of Native American ritual and then moves to physical description. The last two lines, "Mussels clamp to sea-boulders / Sucking the Spring tides" (21), contrast with "Hunting 1," in which "Soft oysters rot now, between tides" (19). The following two-line stanza of "3" names another bird, the duck, and further develops the rainstorm description. The long concluding stanza first adds to that description, then develops the color imagery as the sky darkens in the storm. The "Black Swifts" assume a mythic divinatory role in the closing two lines: "—the swifts cry / As they shoot by, See or go blind!" (21). An ambiguous imperative, it warns that humanity must change its perception in order to "See."

"Hunting 4" opens with an animal-medicine myth and animal-song myths. It then moves more deeply into bird myths, concluding with "Brushed by the hawk's wing / of vision" (22). The narrator has apparently gone on "blind," but the birds help him to gain vision. The next stanza relates a story of the Flathead tribe migrating, which is linked to a bird myth. As Jungels argues, this story may serve to emphasize the importance of accurate naming both in terms of "a fidelity to the text of objects" and "a correspondence to the inner world of myth'' (80); i.e., accuracy in both dimensions of human knowledge.

This segment closes by following this story with a description:

> Raven
> on a roost of furs
> No bird in a bird-book,
> black as the sun. (22)

The narrator of ''Hunting,'' through his increasing perception of birds as mythic creatures, gains an understanding of the limitations of book-knowledge and, by extension, of ''texts'' in general. Snyder ties this perception to a recognition of the most notorious symbolic bird in American literature, the raven, a Northwest trickster figure. Viewing Snyder's physical and mythic portrayals of ''Raven'' in terms of Native American lore, Jungels states that ''the result of these associations, both visual and mythic, is to merge Raven and sun as reciprocal aspects of a single reality embodying both the object and source of vision'' (80). The reality of physical appearance remains a useful source for information, but one that is limited to historical and individual sensory experience. For such experience to be understood and properly acted upon, it must be placed in context by the mythic consciousness of spiritual knowledge.

At the same time that Snyder has carried the poem into a storm's darkness, the blindness of humanity, and the sinister blackness of mythic birds, he has also prepared the reader emotionally for a strong response to the regenerative ritual of ''Hunting 5.'' ''The making of the horn spoon'' presented here is drawn from Kwakiutl ritual (Jungels 82). The ritual shows respect for dead animals by its example of using all their parts; its sacred character is reinforced by the passage closing with an untranslated chant.

''Hunting 8'' opens with a myth-song sung by ''deer,'' a sacred animal. The second stanza describes a hunting experience without redeeming ritual. As a result, the narrator and his cohorts are pursued by the sacred deer, ''howling like a wise man,'' because the

From Myth Criticism to Mythopoeia

deer recognizes the hunter's sacrilege. The second part of ''8'' describes someone driving home drunk, catching a buck in his headlights and shooting it while the buck is blinded, ironically echoing the swifts' warning. The gutting of the deer by the roadside is a debased ritual, as sacrilegious as the first event. The description ends with ''the limp tongue,'' which refers to the loss of the deer's singing voice. This loss represents one danger of ''the future defined,'' in that current American cultural behavior may produce the permanent loss of this voice, both in its physical and mythic roles.

In reading this passage one needs to distinguish the individuals who narrate it. Nothing indicates that the narrative ''I'' of ''Hunting'' as a whole is necessarily the same person who kills the buck. If they are the same person, these incidents are recollections from the narrator's days as a logger. Elsewhere in ''Hunting'' there occur similar narrative shifts suggesting that the narrator of the entire *Myths & Texts* has begun in ''Hunting'' to move beyond the individual ego in his sense of identity. In terms of the text/myth relationship, he is expanding his consciousness beyond his own ego-based experience, his personal text, toward the boundaries of humankind's collective experience. As Dean argues, ''Thus the characteristically Snyderian voice is one in which many voices can be heard.''[12]

The description of wanton murder is followed by a brief epilogue:

> Deer don't want to die for me.
> I'll drink sea-water
> Sleep on beach pebbles in the rain
> Until the deer come down to die
> in pity for my pain. (28)

This promise of penance describes a type of shamanistic journey into the wilderness to seek vision, based on coastal Salish practices. It also suggests the proper relationship between the hunter and the hunted. The vision achieved during this penitential journey is described in "Hunting 9" and "Hunting 10," while "Hunting 11" compares it with the myth of Prajapati, " 'Lord of Creatures' Brahma as Creator," thus linking Western and Eastern visions.[13]

While "Hunting 11" is almost entirely myth and part of a developing process of interpenetrating shamanistic and Hindu-Buddhist myth elements, "12" is entirely text, ostensibly describing the "I" who opens "Hunting" coming out of the mountains after being purified through his wandering. Through the course of "Hunting" this "I" changes from the one who sits by the log-road into a variety of historical and mythical figures who represent different aspects of the narrator's changing perception of humanity's relationship with nature, a key element of his developing consciousness.

Although most of "Hunting" focuses on Native American and shamanistic myths and rituals, "Hunting 11" introduces Prajapati and "14," "15," and "16" expand the integration of Hindu-Buddhist myth elements, linking the two belief systems. This linkage prepares the reader for the predominantly Hindu-Buddhist references in "Burning." "Hunting 16" closes this second major section of *Myths & Texts* with an explicit statement:

> Meaning: compassion
> Agents: man and beasts, beasts
> Got the buddha-nature
> All but
> Coyote. (34)

Uncompassionate Coyote is a savior-figure, derived from Native American mythology, who can serve as an alternative to Christ. Closing "Hunting" with Coyote serves to carry over the mythic Native American beliefs of "Hunting" into the next section. Jungels correctly notes that "in spite of past doubts it is possible to affirm birth and humanness for these are the conditions of compassion" (123).

From Myth Criticism to Mythopoeia

"Burning 1" continues the references to shamanistic experience. The first stanza ends: "Seawater fills each eye" (37), reiterating the theme of vision. The second stanza introduces the Buddhist concept of *karma*—cause and effect or affinity, even across reincarnations—through the image of the infant entering the birth canal, while the third stanza ends: "River recedes. No matter" (37). The distinction between myth and text, ritual and real experience, is undercut by a series of evolutionary and empathetic images in "Burning 1." Humanity has arisen from the mineral and animal life of the planet and must empathetically return to the swamp to "see" the world of which it is a part, but from which it seems apart. Sherman Paul claims that "self-transformation is the work proposed by 'Burning,'" but this overvalues individual achievement.[14] The shaman and the poet are *public* figures, whose transformations serve the community, as emphasized by "Burning 10."

"Burning 2" provides a philosophical gloss of "Burning 1" in its opening stanza. The last line, "Attentive to the real-world flesh and stone" (38), suggests an ironic rejoinder to the word "consciousness." The "consciousness" that sees *only* "the real-world flesh and stone" prevents a person from seeing that "other" within oneself, whether conceptualized in terms of nature, spirit, cultural history, or collective unconscious. Such one-sided sight prevents people from seeing themselves as part of a larger whole and prevents them from being "attentive" in ways beyond rational consciousness. This stanza serves as a response to the reader's anticipated recoil from the identity of "I" and "other" presented in "Burning 1" and presents one philosophical position on the relationship of humanity and nature, self and other.

The second stanza presents a second philosophical position. In response to the rational consciousness that posits the dichotomy of self and "other" (as it is understood in psychoanalytic terms as all that is posited as not part of the self, as alien and often hostile),[15] this stanza posits that the two concepts and the perception of them as a dichotomy are "forms" lacking permanence. The error that produces the dichotomy of consciousness is that of "clinging" to appearances. The final stanza reinforces this recognition through a series of texts demonstrating impermanence Then, Snyder intrudes a reference to books, which pivots the stanza away from the cyclical, nonconscious actions of trees and birds to the conscious actions of people. Such actions lead to thoughts of death, the most conscious reminder of physical impermanence.

"Burning 3," "Maudgalyâyana saw hell," has two stanzas. The first relates the myth of that Buddha's descent to the underworld. Reinvoking sight imagery, line three states: "The mind grabs and the shut eye sees" (39). Snyder uses "mind" rather than consciousness, and the shut eye alludes to the mystical "third eye." The mind moves beyond and below consciousness to gain spiritual vision. The second stanza ends with a description of the mind dropping everything and opening its eyes. This opening does not block out what "the shut eye sees" but unites the two visions. This unity enables the narrator to recognize both the "forms" of the physical world and the "intricate layers of emptiness" of the spiritual world.

"Burning 4" looks to the future as a mythic piece on "Maitreya the future buddha." Although brief, this celebratory passage directly replies to the pessimistic aspect of "Logging 15." Rather than focusing on the cataclysmic end of the kalpa as the solution to the world of "Logging," "Burning 4" focuses on a spiritual rebirth embodied in the promise of a future Buddha.

"Burning 8" quotes an experience of enlightenment John Muir had when he ceased trying to solve a mountain-climbing crisis through conscious analysis: "I seemed suddenly to become possessed / Of a new sense" (44). He experienced *kensho,* in Zen terminology a brief moment of enlightenment, or seeing into "essential nature," enabling him to unite with the rock rather than fight it.[16] The excerpt concludes: "My limbs moved with a positiveness and precision / With which I seemed to have / Nothing at all to do'' (44). The last line suggests both *wuwei,* the action of non-action, and the letting go of consciousness, that release of the self from the limitations of rationality and will, which enables Muir to breach the self/other dichotomy. This text embodies the unity of inner and outer vision mythically propounded in ''Burning 3'' and demonstrates the interpenetration of physical and spiritual realities.

''Burning 10'' presents a humorous sequence of updated Bodhisattva vows, in terms of traditional Buddhist vows being presented in ''Beat'' language, and depictions of physical observations. The last lines echo ''Hunting 12,'' which describes the narrator coming out of the mountains. Here the ''we'' decide not to ''come down'' but to continue ascending. ''Burning 10'' marks a transition in the poem, a commitment to a way of perception that will culminate in the epiphany of ''Burning 17'' in which the dichotomy of myth and text dissolves.

''Burning 11'' and ''Burning 12'' treat the difficulties of embarking on this path. ''11'' imitates koan study in which the student tries to answer the question ''What is the way of non-activity?'' (46). The answer begins with a description of the meditation posture, then blossoms into myth elements, initially beautiful but increasingly presented in terms of pain and fire. It closes with a Coyote-as-savior legend in which he and Earthmaker contemplate rebuilding the world. ''Burning 12'' begins with the narrator describing a nightmarish meditation reiterating the impermanence of the body addressed in ''Burning 2.'' The second stanza tells of ''The City of the Gandharvas,'' a beautiful fairy tale place, but, as Snyder notes, ''an Indian trope for 'a mirage'.''[17] The passage closes with a reference to another bird, the nighthawk, ''Circling & swooping in the still, bright dawn'' (47). These lines underscore the difficulty of experiencing enlightenment along the path of meditation, reiterate the hope that nature will assist in the experiencing of vision, and foreshadow the tranquil state of knowledge presented in ''Burning 17.''

"Burning 13" returns to the more unsure tone opening "Burning 12." The first stanza presents the difficulties of gaining release from the distraction of the senses. The second contrasts the experience of writing poetry, of constructing "little myths," with the text of life in which that writing took place. The third briefly intermixes text and myth fragments, while the fourth begins with a myth of Emperor Wu putting an end to war. This story is brutally contradicted by the lines: "Smell of crushed spruce and burned snag-wood. / remains of men, / Bone-chopped foul remains, thick stew / Food for crows—" (48). The first line alludes to the world of "Logging," while the pun on "foul" (fowl) and the reference to "crows" call into question the vision gained from birds in "Hunting."

The rest of the passage confronts this deepening doubt by acceding that conditions are bad, then responding: "As long as you hesitate, no place to go"—a gloss on the John Muir vignette. After casting doubt on meditation, poetry, and politics, the narrator then defies the darkness:

> It's all vagina dentata
> (Jump!)
> "Leap through an Eagle's snapping beak"

> Actaeon saw Dhyana in the Spring. (49)

He calls on the reader to leap beyond the living of reality to the living of myth, turning the latter into the former to gain a glimpse of the world beyond appearance. The use of the "vagina dentata" and "Dhyana" emphasizes not only the danger of such a leap (Jungels 167) but also the power of myth in its ability to concentrate the essence of experience if one opens oneself to such perception. Snyder punningly alludes to meditation by spelling "Diana" as "Dhyana," which is a transliteration of Sanskrit meaning "absorption; the form of meditation."[18] The passage ends with a

From Myth Criticism to Mythopoeia

haikulike description of a moment of enlightenment, written in the understated language typical of Zen humility.

"Burning 14" also returns to "Burning 10," providing a text of the narrator marrying. "Burning 15" returns this married narrator to civilization. Paul emphasizes correctly that this unity with the "other" is predicated upon an adoption of matrifocal values.[19] The return occurs through a series of locations expanding outward from a farm to the universe, symbolized by its mythic center "Mt. Sumeru L.O." Text and myth alternate until the closing two lines in which they come together as a description of physical reality and as seed for a new mythic vision. After this foreshadowing of "Burning 17," the next passage, "Burning 16," briefly relates a set of songs of different cultures, then reiterates the invocation of "Logging 1," "Dream, Dream, / Earth!" (52). This passage speaks of a human transformation from living a superficial physical reality to living a deep spiritual reality, and closes with the signature of Coyote.[20]

"Burning 17," the final section of "Burning" and of *Myths & Texts,* brings the alternation of myth and text fragments together. It consists not of two stanzas, although initially it seems to, but of three. The first is labeled "the text," the second "the myth," while the third has only three lines:

The sun is but a morning star

Crater Mt. L.O. 1952-Marin-an 1956

end of myths & texts[.] (54)

The first stanza presents a text of fighting a forest fire, one which is extinguished by the predawn rain. The second retells the text as a myth, one which evokes the end of an age: "Fire up Thunder Creek and the mountain— / troy's burning!" and then, "The cloud mutters / The mountains are your mind" (53). The link is made between physical experience and psychological experience, between myth and reality, demonstrating the unity of Snyder's remark that "Myth is a 'reality lived.' . . . Reality is a myth lived."

The myth stanza does not replicate the text stanza. To do so the line "The sun is but a morning star" would need to end the stanza to maintain a parallel with "The last glimmer of the morning star." But Snyder sets the line apart so that it returns the reader to the start of this experience of changed perception, the opening line of "Logging 1." In terms of emotional power, the setting off of this line, taken directly from *Walden,* reverses the ominous tone of the opening and posits unlimited possibility before the reader. The myth presents an awareness the reader can have by recognizing that "the mountains are your mind." This identity is further reinforced by the location line, "Crater Mt. L.O. 1952-Marin-an 1956." The poem has been written as a wandering journey, in which there is no end or goal but only the experience of the journeying itself. The first location, while a physical place, alludes to the Mt. Sumeru of "Burning 15," a mythical, mystical vantage point. "Marin-an 1956" presents the text equivalent, the physical place of Marin County, California; the use of "an," however, allies the location with Zen Buddhism, because this word refers to a Zen temple annex, further reinforcing the allusion to Mt. Sumeru.[21]

The argument for including this location line as part of the sequence is based on considering the poem's final line to be "end of myths & texts." The closing of the sequence represents the end of myths and texts because the reader can no longer view them as separate categories of experience or perception. Snyder's "little myth" of *Myths & Texts* can help readers to learn to recognize the two "sources of human knowledge" as one *myths'n'texts* so they can learn "how to *be* in some specific ecosystem of the far-flung world." The completion of the poem opens up another arm of the spinning galaxy of experience.

Through *Myths & Texts* Snyder not only declares but also works out the public responsibilities of the poet, as well as the contributions of mythopoeia, to the cultural transformation that he believes the United States must undergo. But public responsibilities are only one dimension of a human being, one aspect of being a poet. The poems in *Riprap* written in the final stages and shortly after the composition of *Myths & Texts* emphasize Snyder's personal vision that led him to study Zen Buddhism in Japan.

Notes

1. Gary Snyder, *He Who Hunted Birds in His Father's Village* (Bolinas, Ca.: Grey Fox Press, 1979) x. Further references to this work are given in the text.

2. Tim Dean, *Gary Snyder and the American Unconscious: Inhabiting the Ground* (New York: St. Martin's, 1991).

3. Dean 84–89.

4. On this point, see Snyder's own remarks in Katherine McNeill, *Gary Snyder: A Bibliography* (New York: Phoenix Bookshop, 1983) 8–9.

5. See, for example, Robert Kern, "Clearing the Ground: Gary Snyder and the Modernist Imperative," *Criticism* 19 (Spring 1977) 158–77; Katsunori Yamazato, "Seeking a Fulcrum: Gary Snyder and Japan (1956–1975)," Ph.D. dissertation, University of California, Davis, 1987, 41.

6. Gary Snyder, *Myths & Texts* (1960; rpt. New York: New Directions, 1978) vii. Further references to this work are cited in the text.

7. William J. Jungels, "The Use of Native-American Mythologies in the Poetry of Gary Snyder," Ph.D. dissertation, SUNY at Buffalo, 1973, 214. Further references to this work are cited in the text.

8. Robert Graves, *The White Goddess* (1949; amended and enlarged, New York: Farrar, Straus & Giroux, 1966) 50.

9. Howard McCord, *Some Notes on Gary Snyder's* Myths & Texts (Berkeley: Sand Dollar, 1971) n.p.

10. McCord.

11. As Heinrich Zimmer explains it in *Myths and Symbols in Indian Art and Civilization* (1946; rpt. Princeton: Princeton University Press, 1972) 13–19, a "kalpa" is a single day of the Hindu god Brahma, which lasts for 311,040,000,000,000 human years. Each day consists of four parts or yugas, in which order in the universe declines quarter by quarter. At the end of the cycle the universe undergoes total dissolution and remains in such re-absorption for a Brahma century. And then, the entire cycle begins anew.

12. Dean 123.

13. McCord.

14. Sherman Paul, *In Search of the Primitive: Rereading David Antin, Jerome Rothenberg, and Gary Snyder* (Baton Rouge: Louisiana State University Press, 1986) 241.

15. See Dean for a detailed Lacanian explanation of the "Other."

16. Robert Aitken, *Taking the Path of Zen* (San Francisco: North Point Press, 1982) 140.

17. Snyder quoted by McCord.

18. Aitken 139.

19. Paul 247.

20. In the mid-1980s Snyder commented in correspondence that the second half of "Burning 16" and its use of Coyote is based on language from Smohalla's late-nineteenth-century messianic "Dreaming" religion, which treated Coyote as a future "Messiah." This remark about Coyote as a messiah figure also pertains to his appearances in "Hunting 16" and "Burning 11."

22. See Lok Chua Cheng and N. Sasaki, "Zen and the Title of Gary Snyder's 'Marin-An,' " *Notes on Contemporary Literature* 8.3 (1978) 2–3.

CHAPTER THREE

Working Rhythms: *Riprap & Cold Mountain Poems*

Throughout the 1950s Gary Snyder was publishing poems in various small magazines. After he left for Japan, the submission of his poems, as well as the efforts to get *Myths & Texts* and a collection of short poems published, was largely handled by his friends. Sometimes it would turn out that Philip Whalen or Allen Ginsberg would make poems available to a literary journal and then check with Snyder to see if what they had done was acceptable. There was a good deal of talk among these poets and editors who were publishing the Beats and San Francisco writers about various book and journal projects. Out of such discussions came the publication of Snyder's translations of Han-shan in 1958 in *Evergreen Review* and the collection titled *Riprap* in 1959. These two projects were combined and republished in 1965 under the title *Riprap & Cold Mountain Poems.* A new edition of this volume with an afterword by Snyder was published in 1990.[1]

Riprap, it will be recalled, was Snyder's first book only by circumstance. He was more concerned about having *Myths & Texts* published as a separate book; at the same time, he was amenable to having a collection of his poems printed in conjunction with the works of others or as a separate volume. It is clear from the correspondence available that Snyder did not initially write the poems in *Riprap* to be related or unified in any particular way. At the same time, it is important to recognize that the poems as arranged do represent a sequence. James Wright errs when he remarks that "*Riprap* was a simple collection of occasional poems"; in contrast, Sherman Paul claims that "as always, composition is by book, which is more than the sum of its parts and a greater achievement than any poem."[2] As his small-press publications in the 1950s and the table of contents for *Left Out in the Rain* indicate, Snyder had written dozens of other poems between 1952 and 1958, many of which had been published, that could have gone into *Riprap*. Instead, Snyder elected only twenty-one to appear there, covering his experiences from 1953 through 1958.

These twenty-one poems record a rite of passage, a quest for a personal vision and world understanding, that was initiated in these years. This quest took him from the Western mountains of the United States to Japan and back again, and the arrangement of the poems in *Riprap* both reflects and prefigures the actual journey of Snyder's life from the early 1950s to 1968. The Han-shan translations, or Cold Mountain Poems, actually fall into the middle of Snyder's journey. They were begun in the San Francisco Bay Area while Snyder studied Oriental languages at Berkeley. And, as his knowledge of Buddhism and Asian cultures deepened, he reworked the translations, refining them while he was in Kyoto with the help of a Japanese specialist in Chinese poetry prior to having them published in the *Evergreen Review*. One could argue that the translations ought to be read between the last of the American poems and the first of the Japan poems in the *Riprap* cycle rather than at the end of the volume. Not simply translations, they represent a process of identification and self-actualization experienced by the translator. They help clarify some of Snyder's own poetics in terms of Asian influences, and they clearly show a sense of identification between Snyder and Han-shan, the Cold Mountain poet. At the same time, one should be cautious about drawing biographical conclusions about Snyder by analyzing his depiction of Han-shan.[3]

Working Rhythms

In 1959, Snyder wrote a statement on his poetics for Donald Allen's anthology *The New American Poetry*. There he stated that "I tried writing poems of tough, simple, short words, with the complexity far beneath the surface texture. In part the line was influenced by the five- and seven-character line Chinese poems I'd been reading, which work like sharp blows on the mind."[4] In *Riprap & Cold Mountain Poems,* the poems of Han-shan are examples of just that type of poetry, and one can see in this volume the affinities between the translations and some of the English-language poems. But four of the other poems in the volume come from Snyder's first year in Japan and five others from the experience of working on the tanker *Sappa Creek.* The style, then, of the poems ought to shift if Snyder's claim that they are based on specific places and types of work holds true. And, indeed, to some extent, the poems written in Japan and aboard ship do differ from the others. This accounts for Snyder's own view of the volume as a loose collection, as well as for the complaints of some critics about the uneven quality of the poems.

The first poem of *Riprap,* "Mid-August at Sourdough Mountain Lookout" (3), places the speaker atop a mountain far from civilization. The degree to which this isolation has affected him is suggested by the fact that the pronoun "I" does not appear until the second of this poem's two stanzas; it appears once again in the same line, and that is all. The opening five-line stanza depicts natural events, at first far below with "a smoke haze" down in the valley as a result of "five days rain" followed by three hot days; then closer with pitch glowing on fir-cones; and not too far off, new flies busy swarming. These are facts and processes depicted without emotion or acknowledgment of human presence or point of view. Then, the second stanza begins with the speaker identifying himself in the first person but only by means of a negation: "I cannot remember things I once read." He recalls that he has friends, but they are far off in cities, very different kinds of places.

This place has caused him to establish new points of orientation and identification, but he has not let all ego drop away. Even in his doubt about who this "I" could really be said to be, he is suggesting causal relationships, continuing connections. The place has pulled him loose and away from his past, but it has not abolished it. As the poem moves toward closure, the emphasis is on activity, "drinking" and "looking" as natural actions, part of the nature of the place. This understanding occurs in the "high still air," because it is a place for meditation, for shedding an identity created elsewhere. As Katsunori Yamazato suggests, "the reader feels behind the poem the solitary figure of the young Snyder who . . . is deeply engaged in adjusting the way in which he absorbs the world, his mechanism of perception, and the clarity of the poem directly reflects the quality of the mind that Snyder has attained by this point."[5]

But if the Sourdough summer was a significant period for Snyder learning about himself in relation to the wilderness which he surveyed as fire lookout, the following summer plunged him back into that other world, the one of "cities," alienation, and conflict. The second poem of *Riprap,* "The Late Snow & Lumber Strike of the Summer of Fifty-four" (4–5), also ends with the activity of "looking," but this poem lacks the meditative serenity prompted by Sourdough. Sherman Paul observes that "stillness now hovers over an entire landscape; its psychological equivalent is not serenity but quiet desperation; it tells the absence of work. Hitchhiking is now frantic."[6] Like virtually all of the poems of *Riprap,* these two are highly autobiographical. Snyder had gone up to Washington state in 1954 to start work but after only a few days was laid off. As a result, he had to find work as a logger rather than as a lookout, and this occupation was interrupted by a labor strike.

Snyder opens "Late Snow" with snapshots of conditions in Washington during the strike, depicting himself roaming the state unable to land a job. In the second stanza, he attempts to get back to the Sourdough experience through a quick climb, but the attempt fails. The effort to achieve a moment of tranquility is suggested by the way the lines of the stanza shorten into a haikulike structure, reminiscent of *Myths & Texts*. Pines shrouded in fog appear to float, and the drifting speaker, as unmoored as those pines seem to be, reflects that he can find "No place to think or work." These lines remind one of parts of "Logging," when the poet is depicting the mythic character of the dragon clawing the pines. But the reality there of the Cats killing the forests, as with the reality here of not being able to meditate without also being able to work, thwarts the mythic, idyllic impression sought. The speaker, however, does not despair. Instead, in the third stanza he tries again, by climbing Mt. Baker, and feels a sense of ecstasy, although only momentarily. While on Sourdough in 1953, employed to observe and wait, Snyder could distance himself from the cities and the civilization that was actually making his employment possible. But on Mt. Baker in 1954 he is reminded of that relationship. There is no wilderness without a civilization around it, so he must descend the mountain, where is he caught in a limbo between social labor and individual meditation, to stand in a Seattle unemployment line. In the moment of revelation, as with the first poem, the "I" is finally introduced when recognitions about relationships and mind occur.

Snyder turns, then, for a moment away from the mountains, which he has been turned away from by the economic imperatives of capitalism. The third poem of *Riprap* focuses on a multiplicity of cultures that have existed over time and probes a relationship far more difficult, complex, and complicated than his own problems with finding employment. "Praise for Sick Women" (6–7) looks at perceptions of the menstrual cycle held by a variety of patriarchal cultures. The word "sick" here becomes complicated in its meanings and misunderstandings.

The first stanza of Part 1 presents the stereotype of woman as innately closer to nature, therefore more instinctive and intuitive, but the last line renders the image problematic: "A difficult dance to do, but not in mind.'' Does this last line replicate the anti-intelligence stereotype depicted or does it call that image into question? The difficulty of the dance comes, perhaps, not from a problem with intellect but from a problem in society that requires women to lead their lives in highly structured and strictured patterns. It is not their minds that require them to act *only* emotionally or intuitively but the patriarchal society that has defined them in that way.

The second stanza moves into archetypal imagery that depicts the woman as the cause of male sexuality and the belief that sexuality binds him to the earth and to earthiness. Such a relationship should be a positive result of women's alleged proximity to nature. But as Susan Griffin has demonstrated in *Woman and Nature,* this has not been the case throughout most of the history of Western culture.[7] From early Christianity through the Enlightenment, one finds historical periods in which the dualism of the mind/body split is particularly prominent. The body is viewed as a link to mortality, temptation, sin, and defilement. Therefore, man's relationship to woman is a soul-corrupting one. The temptation of sexuality is clearly evident, but what is it that the man sees? The next single long stanza reveals, through a series of folktales and cultural practices ranging through centuries and across cultures, that he sees the woman menstruating but that he does not see it for the natural event that it is, part of a natural cycle in which he too participates.

Bob Steuding relates that Snyder explained this poem at a poetry reading in 1969 by remarking that he was trying ''to put myself in a place where I could understand the archaic menstrual taboos in regard to the growth and conception of the fetus.'' And Steuding goes on to explain that Snyder ''implies how fear and awe of the procreational process influenced the development of ritual in the hope of controlling the experience.''[8] But what needs also to be emphasized is the degree to which such efforts at male control of the female reflect male efforts at control and domination of nature as well. Both forms of domination result in the stereotyping and denigrating of that which men seek to control.

Crucial to the recognition of the failure of such stereotypes to educate men or women, and to represent reality, is Snyder's repetition of "All women are wounded." This is the kind of notion that denies the natural, cyclical character of the menstrual cycle and sees it as a weakness rather than a sign of strength and fecundity. As with his criticism of Japanese and Chinese cultures in *Myths & Texts*, Snyder here criticizes implicitly primary cultures that demonstrate significant ecological awareness and balance between culture and nature but fail to see the balance inherent in menstruation. When he asks where hell is near the end of the poem and answers that is "in the moon" and then "in a bark shack," he is highlighting through juxtaposition the contradiction between humanity's being a part of and in rhythm with natural cycles and various cultures' denials of that relationship. The hell comes not from the discomfort of cramps but from the social taboos built up around menstruation.

Looking at "Praise for Sick Women" by itself, readers have trouble discerning that Snyder does not accept the various mythologies and cultural beliefs that he presents there. But by reading it along with other poems in *Riprap*, particularly "Milton by Firelight" and "For a Far-Out Friend," it becomes clear that the myths he upholds, as in *Myths & Texts*, are ones that affirm human physicality and the interconnectedness of mind and body, male and female. They are ones that contradict the dualisms that he finds running rampant through the menstrual taboos used to denigrate women.

"Piute Creek" (8) returns the reader to the meditative mood of the first poem in *Riprap* and also speaks against dualistic thinking. The speaker here is in the Yosemite high country and is recording his experience of a tremendous awe-filled moment as he is overwhelmed by the natural world in which he is immersed. Part of this awe results from the abundance of nature in its myriad variations:

> Hill beyond hill, folded and twisted
> Tough trees crammed
> In thin stone fractures
> A huge moon on it all, is too much.

Besides filling the speaker with awe, this moment also induces a sense of what the poet Robinson Jeffers called, in the preface to *The Double Axe and Other Poems,* the "transhuman magnificence." Nature includes and surrounds the individual, and in the process of realizing that participatory inclusion, he moves beyond the limitations of being human. Human here does not mean homo sapiens so much as it means civilized people, those who have separated themselves from wild nature through culture, technology, and behavior.

> All the junk that goes with being human
> Drops away, hard rock wavers
> . . . .
> Words and books
> Like a small creek off a high ledge
> Gone in the dry air.

The key concepts here are the wavering of the rock and the simile comparing books to flowing water. In the first instance, the sense of natural entities as solid, static objects—things as resources, inert except for human use—breaks down. They are seen in their process, their activity that comprises all of nature as an interactive, dynamic web of energy transfers. In the second instance, the forgetting of that book-knowledge which is irrelevant, trivial, and inaccurate is depicted as itself a natural process of learning. The behaviors of the creek and the speaker result from the specific conditions of dry summer days in the Sierras.[9]

The second stanza of "Piute Creek" pulls back from this immersion to work out the experience as a lesson. And this stanza renders it a different kind of poem from "Mid-August at Sourdough.'' That poem depicted the process of meditation and its implications but drew no specific lessons. What Snyder has learned at Piute Creek is summarized in the first three lines of this second stanza: ''A clear, attentive mind / Has no meaning but that / Which sees is truly seen.'' One's vision is based on one's place when experiencing that vision. One can see a similar relationship posited in much more mythical terms in the ''Hunting'' section of *Myths & Texts,* particularly in the various bird passages. But Snyder has not yet finished the poem. To leave it here would, if only by force of human habit, give the impression that nature still exists for people since it is a person who is doing all this seeing. But even as one could say that a human looking at Piute Creek is civilized nature studying wild nature, the reverse can occur. Snyder introduces to the poem the belief that wild nature in its various manifestations can and does see and study human nature:

> Back there unseen
> Cold proud eyes
> Of Cougar or Coyote
> Watch me rise and go.

At the end Snyder is also remarking on the fact that the speaker is but a visitor to this particular part of wild nature, not a resident. It is appropriate, then, that he approach the place not only with awe but also with deference to its inhabitants.

''Milton By Firelight'' (9–10), with the dateline ''Piute Creek, August 1955,'' continues the same process of lesson learning but does so in the course of attacking some of the myths that make it difficult for humanity to learn the ways of wild nature. The poem begins with a dismal quotation from Milton's *Paradise Lost* and then contrasts that with the portrait of a man utterly in tune with ''The vein and cleavage'' of the rocks he works with building trails. Looking at this man in place, Snyder concludes, ''What use, Milton, a silly story,'' rejecting in its entirety the Genesis account of Adam and Eve's expulsion from the Garden of Eden.

The next stanza describes an Indian, who, like the rock worker, is in place and hungry for fresh "tomatoes and green apples." There is no temptation here, and no loss of innocence. Being from a different culture, he need not be subjected to Christian mythology. As Thomas Leach suggests, referentiality not symbolism is what concerns the poet at this point: "An apple for Snyder is a real fruit, not a symbol of supernatural knowledge."[10] From the observation of this "chainsaw boy," Snyder is led to an observation about temporality and the relationship of human time to biospheric time. Recognizing that the land surrounding him will eventually dry up to the point where it cannot sustain human life, he concludes that there never was a "paradise" or a "fall." According to Snyder, the acceptance of human mortality and the much greater longevity of the mountains frees humanity from both the desire for paradise—the utopian idealization of the unattainable—and the abhorrence of hell—the demonic idealization of human fallibility.

At the end of this third stanza, the speaker utters the epithet "OH HELL!," but it is only an expression of frustration. Hell may be a state of mind, a sense of damnation that people genuinely experience, but it is not part of the natural world except as nightmare. The final stanza places Milton and the speaker's wrestling with his own words in proper perspective. "Fire down" is a real event, the fading of the campfire, but it also may be metaphor for the dying down of the kind of Puritanical mind Milton exemplifies. And in the end, the speaker accepts Milton's imaginings and the myth he promotes as part of human participation in the world. If humanity's stay in the Sierras is temporal, eventually giving way to the scorpion, then the kind of concerns Milton espouses, and some of the speaker's contemporaries share, must also eventually pass away. The speaker and Milton are both seeking to understand the world in which they find themselves, but they are using different myths to do it. Snyder has passed judgment on Milton's beliefs and the Christian myth of the Fall, but his tone changes from anger and frustration at the beginning of the poem to an acceptance of the existence of such beliefs and a recognition of their temporality at poem's end.

"Above Pate Valley" and "Water" (11 and 12), the two poems that follow "Milton by Firelight," continue to address the issue of temporality by representing the specific events of two separate summer days. In neither case is there the kind of commentary found in "Piute Creek" and "Milton by Firelight." Instead, the direct experience of the thing itself is presented. Human temporality is depicted in the first poem by the speaker's finding thousands of arrowhead shavings, indicating that Native Americans had camped where the speaker now camps. There is, then, a continuity of human experience but also a recognition of differences. Snyder knows he is not Indian and cannot replicate that life, but must pursue his own way into human/nature harmony: "They came to camp. On their / Own trails. I followed my own / Trail here. . . . " At the same time, the last line of the poem, "Ten thousand years," seems to honor the presence of a humanity in this place that has known how to act accordingly, leaving little trace and less damage. Continuity and discontinuity, change and permanence abide together in this experience.

"Water" depicts a unique experience. The speaker dunks himself into a fast-flowing mountain stream and, with "ears roaring," "Eyes open," and head "aching from the cold," finds himself facing a trout. The suggestion is that of an experience undergone in a state of ecstasy, as implied by the dancing, leaping run of the speaker, mimicked by the lineation and sounds of this single-stanza poem. Here there is total immersion without separate consciousness, both literally through the head ducking and figuratively through the indication that the nature of the place compelled the speaker to act in this manner. He claims that the sun "Whirled" him into his descent while a baby rattlesnake forced him to leap.

But more can be read into this poem if one recalls that in "Mid-August at Sourdough" the speaker is "drinking cold snow-water." He has moved from meditation to a state of ecstatic immersion in nature. That first poem and this one can be seen to frame a certain journey or passage from one level of consciousness to another or from the beginning of a new level of consciousness about humanity-in-nature to its fulfilled awareness. Compared with the "unseen" animal observers of "Piute Creek," this fish meets the speaker eyeball to eyeball in a more equal relationship as the human enters its medium.

The next two poems focus on meeting two people very different from one another, but in both cases Snyder addresses the issue of possibilities and probable futures. The four poems following these address various topics but all seem focused on decision-making processes. Like "Piute Creek," they are more about the one seeing than the seen. They are followed by the Japan poems of *Riprap* and one cannot help but think of them in terms of Snyder's biography. The months between the end of the Yosemite work and Snyder's first trip to Japan were ones of preparation for departure. Perhaps most interesting here is the range of tones and the subtle but unmistakable expression of conflicting emotions in these poems.

"For A Far-Out Friend" (13–14) takes the reader back to "Praise for Sick Women," in part because this is the second poem in which women are mentioned and in part because of the subject of mythological depictions of women and the feminine. Sickness comes up again in this poem, but here it is the sickness of the speaker, specifically a lack of sanity resulting from his participation in the male chauvinism of American patriarchal culture and its violence against women. And here is a curious contradiction. The poem presents a recognition of the dangers of idealization at the same time that the speaker engages in idealizing a woman by identifying her with images of Hindu goddesses. The reason for his violence toward her remains unstated, and, while recognizing a certain superiority on her part because she "had calm talk" for him, the speaker wants her to share the blame for the situation.

The first stanza concludes with the speaker thinking back to an earlier time of ecstasy between him and the woman, and he remarks, "I saw you as a Hindu Deva-girl." In the second stanza, he claims that visions of her body made him "high" for weeks. He tells her that he found in "Zimmer's book of Indian Art" pictures of Hindu stone statues that reminded him of her as he remembered her running through the surf. From this idealization and mythologizing of her "body," he is pulled down to earth by a sudden recognition:

> And I thought—more grace and love
> In that wild Deva life where you belong
> Than in this dress-and-girdle life
> You'll ever give
> Or get.

What remains unclear at the end is the degree to which the speaker recognizes his own complicity. Does he realize that he too has been part of that "dress-and-girdle life" through his violence and through his idealization of her physical attributes as displaying some divine essence? Further, the problem of falling back on mythology to stereotype women, even when the stereotypes are allegedly positive and beatific, seems unrecognized.[11] The images employed by Snyder in this poem of the Deva girl may seem part of a positive depiction of women, but they actually feed into the kind of stereotypes that he criticizes in "Praise for Sick Women." In neither poem are real women engaged by the speaker. Charlene Spretnak makes an interesting remark in this regard: "I think the full capacity for valuing the radical female voice arose within Gary only at midlife. . . . The women in the early works are often presented as slightly alien creatures who are perceived to be in an adversarial relationship, at some level, to the poet."[12] One can in the context of *Riprap* profitably read this poem as the demonstration, perhaps unintentional, of the limitations of the speaker's developing consciousness. These limitations are manifested in two ways. One, while he has been working out the relationship of human to wild nature, he has clearly not learned much about the relationship of human to human when gender is involved. Two, he has not figured out how to mediate the contradictions between his budding vision of an appropriate relationship of human to nature and the violent, destructive characteristics of modern American society.

"Hay for Horses" (15) is a much simpler poem, basically the narrative of an old man who has found himself performing the same work his whole life and being dissatisfied with it the entire time. Although the situation has positive aspects, as indicated by the description of loading the hay into the barn, the poem clearly shows the dangers of being locked in for life by the necessities of labor. In this sense, although tonally much lighter, it echoes elements of "The Late Snow."

"Thin Ice" (16) seems to follow in the same vein. Snyder describes an experience in which the figurative language of an old saying, "Like walking on thin ice," is depicted as a literal event. If read in relation to "Hay for Horses," it suggests that that poem is not just a story but perhaps also a warning for the speaker. In terms of Snyder's life, what if he had decided, after all, not to go to Japan, but had stayed in California drifting from one temporary job to another or becoming a permanent trail crew member? The poem also suggests that people don't take folk wisdom and myths seriously enough, forgetting that such stories are based on real, and often painful, experience. "Piute Creek" and "Milton by Firelight" could be read in this light too, in terms of the distinction between the wisdom of the actual experiences related in the poems versus the imagined experience of Milton's epic.

There is also the common occurrence of people knowing something but perhaps not really taking it to heart. "Nooksack Valley" (17) has a little of this experience in it, in terms of the mood of ambivalence and uncomfortable waiting that is implied. The speaker is observing the valley around him, but he is not really paying attention to it. Instead, he is thinking of the near future when he will return to San Francisco and then depart for Japan.

But this thought does not produce euphoria or even happiness. The poet looks back with doubt and uncertainty. He realizes how much he loves the land he has come to know intimately, and feels a certain premature nostalgia for the positive aspects of America's young culture. He also doubts his own development, speaking of "wasted theories," "schools, girls, deals," and writing bad poetry. These lines suggest another of those moments in Snyder's life when he doubted his vocation as a poet or doubted the efficacy of poetry as a force for cultural change and the raising of consciousness.

The irony, of course, is that this doubt about poetry is expressed in a carefully crafted poem, with close attention to line breaks, phrasing, and the layout of the poem on the page. That this doubt is couched in a larger recognition that, for better or worse, the speaker is a poet, is indicated by the behavior of the dog who is described at the close of the poem: after turning about in circles, he settles down to sleep. At a certain point the speaker has to quit doubting and worrying and take the next step regardless of the risk and difficulties it entails. In the meantime, he may as well get some rest. Such a conclusion is reinforced by the following poem, "All Through the Rains" (18), which describes the independent behavior of a mare that the speaker tries, and fails, to catch and ride.

"Migration of Birds" (19) serves as a rejoinder to "Nooksack Valley." Here the speaker is resolved and recognizes that different people have different paths, even as the birds migrate along their own separate patterns. A hummingbird pulls the speaker into the world and out of his book. He thinks of other birds, then of another human. Snyder's friend Jack Kerouac, who shared Snyder's cabin in Mill Valley for a while, is brought into the poem. An interesting contrast is established. Kerouac, who will remain in the United States although professing an interest in Japan and Buddhism, is reading *The Diamond Sutra*, a Buddhist text in translation. Snyder, in contrast, the day before, read *Migration of Birds,* a book about nature. The speaker remarks that "Today that big abstraction's at our door," the abstraction in this case being the book that he's read, which uses words to convey the idea of the birds' observable behavior. *The Diamond Sutra* too is an abstraction, being read by Kerouac out of context and treated only as a text. Snyder will soon be at Buddhism's door, beginning an experiential rather than textual study. The speaker identifies with the migration of birds leaving the San Francisco Bay Area. He implies that, while the nostalgia felt in "Nooksack Valley" may result from realizing the Pacific West is his home, Japan may be an equally appropriate nesting place. And that implies, in turn, that his own natural cycle of migration will bring him back to the States.

But for now, Japan will become his focus. Despite the importance of this first trip to Japan for Snyder, given that it afforded him a range of important insights sufficient to keep him returning for nearly twelve years, he provides the reader with only four poems (there is a similar dearth of poems from this period in *Left Out in the Rain* as well). But there is a very clear reason for this. As Snyder has remarked many times, when he meditates he does not think about poetry, and in Japan he became intensely focused on his Buddhist practice. He also had to work on his Japanese, both to speak the language and to engage in the translation work expected of him by the First Zen Institute of America. He also saw a contradiction between his poetry and his studies.

The Japan poems, even though there are only four, do significantly contribute to the volume. "Toji" (20) depicts the extremely relaxed atmosphere he discovered in a "Shingon temple" in Kyoto. As he concludes, "Nobody bothers you in Toji." Snyder depicts not only the relaxed behavior of the people in the temple compound but also the very different kind of statues of gods found there. This depiction stands in stark contrast to his portrayal of the only other religious tradition previously mentioned in *Riprap,* Milton's Puritan Christianity. Clearly, Snyder wants to impart to the reader a sense of freedom and flexibility that he discovered shortly after arrival in Kyoto. Sherman Paul believes that the use of "shadow" and "shade" implies that this flexibility relates in particular to an acceptance of the unconscious, which in turn would suggest a less repressed attitude toward sexuality.[13]

In the second poem, "Higashi Hongwanji" (21), which is a "Shinshu temple," Snyder again depicts a temple interior, but the people present are treated in only a single line. He focuses instead on a "carved wood panel" high up behind a beam that reminds the speaker of the sexuality found throughout nature. This attention to sexuality is also the focus of "Kyoto: March" (22), but is addressed for the first time in *Riprap* in terms of familial ties and multigenerational love. The winter weather described through most of the poem serves primarily as background for the brief but extremely tender attention given first to the lovers who untangle their bodies at dawn and then "wake and feed the children," as well as the grandchildren, whom they love. Here human nature and wild nature are intertwined, as are the lovers, in a relationship rendered sacred to the speaker by its ordinariness and its repetition.

"A Stone Garden" (23–25) develops this relationship of human and wild nature further, with the recognition that Japan's highly organized society and well-cultivated nature retain some of the values Snyder had previously only found in the wilderness. The word "stone" in the title connects it with the previous trail-building poems of Yosemite and with the final poem "Riprap." "A Stone Garden" definitely does not embody the riprap rhythms of the earlier poems. Rather, it is much more formal, and hence more gardenlike, than the wilderness poems. But, despite the complaints of some critics, this formalism is just as organic as the riprap poetics in the sense that the organization of the poem embodies the orderliness and structured relationships that Snyder finds in his subject matter.

In the first stanza, Snyder intermingles real and dream images of Japan, reflecting in part his own process of idealizing, dreaming about, Japan and experiencing its realities firsthand. There is also a sense of historical continuity, the kind of mythic linkages associated with dream time, transmitted through rural agricultural practices. As Sherman Paul notes, "the culture that he depicts here gives woman and domestic life a central place, . . . founds itself on *eros* and *ecos*."[14] But the speaker is clearly only observer and dreamer rather than participant; that this distinction matters is suggested by the fact that Snyder chooses to provide the reader with the location for the writing of the poem, the Red Sea, far from Japan and the experience depicted.

The second stanza treats the familial relationships already appreciated in "Kyoto: March." Here they receive the same idealized treatment, with an emphasis again on multigenerational love and extended families. Added to this is an acceptance of aging and dying. Snyder then claims that "time is destroyed." As the lines that follow that expression indicate, "time," in the sense of movement and passage, continues. But since it is recognized as more cyclical than linear, the destructive perceptions that people have of aging and dying, perceptions that produce misery, despair, and self-loathing, are banished. The individual is not the be-all or end-all of life, but rather part of the web of life, knit together in relationship with love, which is the continuation of humanity.

Those perceptions, however, prove inadequate to the nostalgia and loneliness the speaker feels as a result of remaining an outsider. In the third stanza, in highly stylized rhyming lines, Snyder compares the insignificance of the individual poet trying to fill the void with words and music when "The noise of living families fills the air." If one thinks of Romantic poetry as it is commonly portrayed—an individual speaking to himself, standing alone in the world and overheard only by the reader—then it makes sense that such poetry does not compare to conversation based on love. For poetry to have meaning, it must establish or continue a dialogue, a relationship with others.

Lack of such dialogue and relationship is precisely what is regretted at the start of the final section of "A Stone Garden." But

Snyder turns away from this regret and emphasizes instead the possibility of family based on observation of its realization in Japan. He concludes the final stanza to the fourth section and the poem as a whole: "Allowing such distinctions to the mind: / A formal garden made by fire and time." Families and relationships are not simply realized and stumbled into but are built through passion and patience. The speaker must maintain these even in his moments of loneliness and isolation, if he is to be prepared to experience human love in the future. That there is hope has been suggested throughout by imagery and allusion, such as the real girl who opens the second section, or the allusions to "Narihira's lover" and the "long-lost hawk." The depiction of the girl reminds the knowledgeable reader of a relationship in the ninth-century Japanese volume, *The Tales of Ise,* while the allusions refer to an eighth-century poem by Yakamochi on falconry which relates the story of a lost falcon. In that poem, a maid appears to the falconer "telling him not to be worried, for it would return to him."[15]

The next five poems of *Riprap* treat the *Sappa Creek* tanker days, based on the time Snyder spent on that ship earning money for his mother and working his way back to the United States from Japan in a roundabout journey. The first three poems are largely descriptive, showing Snyder orienting himself toward this strange new situation, fully aware of the contrast, as indicated in "At Five A. M." (27), between machine life and plant life. "T-2 Tanker Blues" and "Cartagena" (29–30 and 31), however, are rich poems similar to "Kyoto: March" and "A Stone Garden." In the first of these, Snyder is working through the mythic implications of the contradictions between East and West and between human nature and wild nature. In what sounds like a response to Robinson Jeffers's doctrine of Inhumanism, which he defined in *The Double Axe* as humanity moving beyond egocentrism, Snyder states: "I will not cry Inhuman & think that makes us small and nature / great." Here he is clearly expanding on the newfound appreciation for humanity in its diversity that he first began to realize in Japan.

The immersion in immediacy expressed toward the end of "T-2" also suggests an emphasis on the present moment, on the *tathata* or suchness of the world in its Buddhist sense, when he compares "Mind & Matter" with the foam on a glass of beer. Although some critics hear a tone of sadness and depression because of the lines preceding these, these lines are, rather, simple recognitions, a letting go of the objects and problems that have earlier possessed and troubled the poet's mind. As Thomas Leach notes, "the mood of nostalgia yields to an air of detachment in which human life becomes simply another facet in the ever-shifting kaleidoscopic pattern of nature."[16]

"Cartagena" seems to share this tone as well. Snyder speaks here of the virtually mindless, frenzied behavior of himself and his fellow seamen on an overnight shoreleave, engaging in sex without love, commodity exchange rather than familial relationship. And he recalls a similar experience when he was a seaman that summer after his graduation from high school—thus the dateline "Colombia 1948—Arabia 1958." Virtually nothing has changed from one event to the other except time and place. The events are a reality that cannot be encompassed simply by an appeal to religion, as suggested by Snyder's drunken mouthing of a phrase from St. Augustine, who converted from paganism to Christianity. They occur and continue occurring, part of the life that can only be studied in the process of experiencing it rather than as a substitute for experiencing it.

Such temporality and contingency prepare the reader for the final, title poem, "Riprap" (32), which speaks of how to live as well as how to write and read poetry. Poetry as a material thing, in the form of the written poem, the performed text, and as a relationship, forms part of the world in which humans find themselves and is a source of clues by which they may interpret that world and their place in it. But place is also a relationship, an activity, a "Game of *Go*." This poem, while embodying in its theme and form the aesthetic concepts displayed throughout *Riprap,* also embodies a way to learn the world, and a world by which to learn the way. This way is nothing short of "being-in-the-world," a constantly transitory process. It is crucial to realize that the *Riprap* collection ends with an emphasis not on coming to terms with the world but on the recognition that the world constantly changes, and humans must change their perceptions to keep pace. As Snyder says in his afterword to the 1990 edition of *Riprap & Cold Mountain Poems,* "the title . . . celebrates the work of hands, the placing of rock, and my first glimpse of the image of the whole universe as interconnected, interpenetrating, mutually reflecting, and mutually embracing" (65–66).

This recognition of interconnection may be partly responsible for Snyder's assuming the task of writing another long sequential poem, *Mountains and Rivers without End,* more complex and with more interconnecting, interpenetrating components than *Myths & Texts.* Similarly, interconnection enables him to see the need and the way to return to the United States, bearing his own eclectic wisdom with him as a teaching instrument for the new directions he saw American culture taking in the 1960s.

Notes

1. Gary Snyder, *Riprap and Cold Mountain Poems* (San Francisco: North Point Press, 1990). All page references given in the text are to this edition. Snyder relates the publication history of this volume in his afterword.

2. Crunk (James Wright), "The Work of Gary Snyder," *The Sixties* 6 (Spring 1962); rpt. in James Wright, *Collected Prose,* ed. Anne Wright (Ann Arbor: University of Michigan Press, 1983) 108; Sherman Paul, *In Search of the Primitive: Rereading David Antin, Jerome Rothenberg, and Gary Snyder* (Baton Rouge: Louisiana State University Press, 1986) 214.

3. For those interested in analyses of the Han-shan poems, both in terms of Snyder's own development and in comparison with other translations and with Chinese poetic tradition, see the following: Lee Bartlett, "Gary Snyder's Han-Shan," *Sagetrieb* 2 (1983) 105–10; Ling Chung, "Whose Mountain Is This?—Gary Snyder's Translation of Han Shan," *Renditions* 7 (Spring 1977) 93–102; Paul Kahn, *Han Shan in English* (Buffalo: White Pine Press, 1989); Jacob Leed, "Gary Snyder, Han Shan, and Jack Kerouac," *Journal of Modern Literature* 11 (1984) 185–93;

Understanding Gary Snyder

Yao-fu Lin, " 'The Mountains Are Your Mind': Orientalism in the Poetry of Gary Snyder," *Tamkang Review* 6–7 (1975–1976) 357–91.

4. Donald M. Allen, ed., *The New American Poetry* (New York: Grove Press, 1960) 420–21.

5. Katsunori Yamazato, "Seeking a Fulcrum: Gary Snyder and Japan (1956–1975)," Ph.D. dissertation, University of California, Davis, 1987) 32.

6. Paul 215.

7. Susan Griffin, *Woman and Nature: The Roaring Inside Her* (New York: Harper & Row, 1978).

8. Bob Steuding, *Gary Snyder* (Boston: Twayne, 1976) 141.

9. See Tim Dean, *Gary Snyder and the American Unconscious: Inhabiting the Ground* (New York: St. Martin's, 1991) 169, for a very different reading of these lines.

10. Thomas J. Leach, Jr., "Gary Snyder: Poet as Mythographer," Ph.D. dissertation, University of North Carolina at Chapel Hill, 1974, 8.

11. See Paul 219.

12. Charlene Spretnak, "Dinnertime," in *Gary Snyder: Dimensions of a Life*, ed. Jon Halper (San Francisco: Sierra Club Books, 1991) 361.

13. Paul 220.

14. Paul 223.

15. Sanehide Kodama, *American Poetry and Japanese Culture* (Hamden, Ct.: Archon Books, 1984) 182–83.

16. Leach 35; cf. Charles Molesworth, *Gary Snyder's Vision: Poetry and the Real Work* (Columbia: University of Missouri Press, 1983) 20.

CHAPTER FOUR

Of Mountains, Rivers, and Back Country: *Six Sections from Mountains and Rivers without End Plus One* and *The Back Country*

Six Sections from Mountains and Rivers without End Plus One

S hortly after completing *Myths & Texts,* Snyder began work on another long poetic sequence, *Mountains and Rivers without End.* To this day, Snyder continues working on it and promising to complete it. Over the years he has published nearly two dozen individual pieces, but only twice has he collected any of them into book form. In 1965, he published *Six Sections from Mountains & Rivers without End* and, then, in 1970 published *Six Sections from Mountains and Rivers without End Plus One.*[1] The first version comprises five poems previously published in journals between 1961 and 1965, plus "The Elwha River." The 1970 edition adds to these "The Blue Sky," originally published in 1968.

Snyder considers all of these poems "drafts" open to revision in the process of completing the book, and he has discouraged critics from drawing conclusions about the entire sequence. Snyder remarked in 1983:

> On the ecological level, *Mountains and Rivers* sets up a real biosphere poem. One of my insights in my recent years of ecological thought is that the precise knowledge of what we call

"local" knowledge results in the understanding of limits that goes with localness. . . . That kind of knowledge has to be transformed into a planetary scale. . . .

. . . . *Mountains and Rivers* points in that direction, it tries to leap from the local to the planetary level and back again.[2]

Clearly, Snyder did not have this understanding when he began the sequence. While its structure may have been envisioned from the beginning, its thematic base has evolved, and such development necessarily interacts with the structure. In 1989, Snyder responded to a question about *Mountains and Rivers:* "It is not easy to say where it stands. . . . I don't know what shape it will take until I lay it all out again."[3]

The inconclusiveness of *Six Plus One,* both in terms of its being part of a larger whole and its open-to-revision character, compounds the difficulties of comprehension for any reader. The individual poems are difficult because, like *Myths & Texts,* they are highly allusive and elliptical. Readers picking up *Six Plus One* as their first Snyder volume may very well find it impenetrable.[4] Snyder is aware of this problem but hopes that the interrelations among all of the twenty-five to forty sections will illuminate the more esoteric and cryptic passages.[5]

The structure of the sequence will possibly be based on the classical Japanese Noh play *Yamauba* by Seami,[6] an author mentioned by Snyder in *Myths & Texts.* According to Bob Steuding, this means that the sequence, like Noh, will be "basically constructed around the journey motif"; in the *Yamauba,* he continues, "where the title 'Mountains and Rivers Without End' finds its inception, 'hills,' meaning mountains, represent life; and one's travels in these hills, in terms of the Buddhist 'Wheel of Life,' are the endless round of reincarnation."[7] But even interpretation of the title is complicated by the fact that in Chinese the characters for "mountains" and "rivers" when placed together form the ideogram for "landscape." Mountains and rivers is also a particular genre of

Chinese landscape painting, frequently done on long scrolls. Rather than attempt a comprehensive interpretation of all seven poems of *Six Plus One,* this chapter will discuss only the highlights of them before turning to Snyder's *The Back Country.*

In "Bubbs Creek Haircut," the opening poem,[8] Snyder begins with a first-person autobiographical narrator preparing for a journey. Such an opening follows the Noh tradition. Snyder's speaker gets a haircut before entering the mountains, and it turns out that the barber has been where this speaker intends to go. In the second stanza, reality unravels a bit in the Goodwill Store. Discarded items are described as having lives of their own and the proprietor is referred to as "The Master of the limbo drag-legged," invoking the mythic image of a limping god. Snyder establishes a mood of expectancy, indicating that this journey represents a crucial quest.

The next few stanzas begin the actual journey and initiate a process of interweaving memories, presenting events in a collapsing of time and space. Attachments are being dropped away in the same way that the speaker sheds his hair; the implication that the haircut was a preparatory ritual is reinforced here, its being akin to the shaving of Buddhist acolytes' heads in imitation of the Guatama Buddha. And that story suggests something to the reader about the barber, since it was not a man but the Hindu god Vissakamma who shaved the Buddha. The story of the head-shaving is known as *maha-ahiniskramana,* "the great departure."[9] Quickly Snyder brings the reader to a vastly different land, one of "a half-iced over lake, twelve thousand feet" that is "the realm of fallen rock" (1). He warns readers that they have reached a world of spirits in which the laws of the city no longer apply and in which visions may be experienced. The lake and its flowing waters depicted in this stanza both return the reader to the title of the sequence and symbolize the concept of the universal womb, network of energy, through which all material entities pass. This symbolism is made explicit by the line that closes the stanza.

But in order to reach this lake, the speaker has had to involve himself in a series of human and economic exchanges, embodiments of the abstract concept of "goodwill." The experiences with his friends Locke and A[llen] G[insberg] are divided by the memory of a failed haircut. The reality of segregation related in this haircut story indicates that goodwill is not yet universal. His final exchange involves being drafted to carry messages between trail crew camps.

The observation of the "deva world" mountain lake—i.e., a place filled with good spirits—leads the narrator into a strange meditation, first referring to the Goodwill proprietor as "King of Hell" and then moving into a celebration of the dance of "moon breast Parvati," who is both the consort of the Hindu god Shiva (frequently depicted as a dancer) and an earth goddess figure.[10] Anthony Hunt views the entrance of Parvati as a moment of revelation in which Snyder realizes that his path to enlightenment will go not by the route of being a world-renouncing mountain ascetic—perhaps in the likeness of Han-shan—but by the route of Tantra and immersion in the physicality of the world.[11] In order to do this, he must recognize the total interpenetration of all of nature. Thus at the end of his ecstatic meditation, he is able to see the equivalence of objects in the Goodwill basement and the wild nature around him in the mountains:

> a room of empty sun or peaks and ridges
>   beautiful spirits,
>
>   rocking lotus throne:
> a universe of junk, all left alone. (4)

The end phrase does not signal ascetic withdrawal, since that would contradict the social interaction occurring throughout the poem, but acceptance of a viewpoint that recognizes all is interconnected and simultaneously unique.

The next section returns to everyday memories that reiterate the theme of goodwill: the narrator getting a ride because a trucker recognized his green hat; his meeting up with the other trail crew and delivering one message and receiving another in return. But all this ends with a revealing parenthesis:

> (on Whitney hair on end
> hail stinging barelegs in the blast of wind
> but yodel off the summit echoes clean). (5)

One not only can have visions in the mountains but also can experience the purification that comes from the recognition of a deep spiritual lesson.

The poem then moves to a conclusion revealing that the haircut which began the poem also happened long ago, that "all this" recounted in the poem "came after," including the memory of the haircut in which the poet recognizes its deeper significance. And that significance is contained in the return to "the double mirror waver" of the barbershop's mirrors (6). Snyder informed Ekbert Faas, when explaining "Bubbs Creek Haircut," that "multiple reflections in multiple mirrors, that's what the universe is like."[12] This is not Snyder's own trope but one that arises from a well-known story about the Chinese master Fa-Tsang trying to explain the Hua-Yen Buddhist doctrine of interpenetration to the Empress Wu Tse-Tien. In that story he designs a totally mirrored room to display infinite reflections of the Buddha-figure set in its middle.[13] In like manner, Snyder has designed a totally mirrored poem in which the mirrors that begin and end the poem reflect, through the medium of the poet's memories, the interpenetration of events across space and time.

Snyder provides the date for the poem's composition at the end, "April 4, 1960." It was written, then, not when the poet was immersed in the Sierras but when he was immersed in *sanzen,* formal Buddhist meditation, in Kyoto. What is perhaps most interesting is that it records Snyder's poetic depiction of a moment of sudden enlightenment about a crucial Buddhist teaching a few months before he had just such an experience in his own life, June 11 of that year. He wrote to Katsunori Yamazato: "I was shelving books in the stacks of the Ryosen-an library, and while pushing a book into its place suddenly and totally saw myself together with all other entities of the universe, each totally 'in place' and beautifully so."[14] "Bubbs Creek Haircut," based upon the poet's own experiences, opens up to the reader a new way of perceiving the world that breaks through physical appearances and rationalist constructs, suggesting a set of relationships by which that world works different from the ones dominant in American culture.

The second poem in *Six Plus One,* "The Elwha River," makes it evident that other visionary experiences will follow as it opens with "I was a girl waiting by the roadside for my boyfriend to come" (7). The interpenetration of the reality of dreams and the reality of waking experiences gradually becomes clear as the theme of this first section. The complex interconnections of dreams, memories, and memories within dreams suggest that both dreams and recollections are prone to error in relation to the natural world. But at the same time, both may also be accurate in establishing a balanced human relationship with that natural world, regardless of the "facts." After all, if the body is part of nature, then both recollections and dreams are "mirrors" of nature reflecting it and each other. This interdependence is reinforced in "The Elwha River" by Snyder providing part one with its date of origin, "21.X.1958," and the other two parts of the poem with their own date, "21.VIII.1964." A dream and its written record become shaping parts of a poem completed six years later.

"Night Highway Ninety-Nine" is clearly a poem that stands on its own in the sense of being thematically understandable without reference to the rest of the sequence. Like "Bubbs Creek Haircut," it was written in Japan. And, according to a letter to Philip Whalen, Snyder views it at his "traveling song," an opening component of the traditional Noh play.[15] This tradition of the "traveling song" clarifies the connection between hitchhiking and certain kinds of Buddhist practice. A close-to-home example for Snyder of such practice is the monk named in part two, Sokei-An, the Japanese Zen master who wandered the Pacific Northwest in the early 1900s and who was instrumental in the establishment of the First Zen Institute of America. Even though "Night Highway" is structured according to the sequence of the towns the poet passes through, it weaves together experiences spread over an array of years. And when Snyder names "the Goodwill" in part three, it becomes evident that all of these exchanges bear the imprint of that previous theme. Similarly, allusions to Buddhism and other religious practices are interlaced throughout the sections. In particular, the notion of breaking through the illusion of permanence and the appearance of solidity of things is emphasized, as when the narrator remarks in part five: "The road that's followed goes forever; / In half a minute crossed and left behind" (21).

While some critics have praised Snyder's "Hymn to the Goddess San Francisco in Paradise," it is the most troubling and weakest in *Six Plus One* because of its sexism. As in "Praise for Sick Women" and "For a Far-Out Friend" in *Riprap,* Snyder relies on a mythological treatment of a positive ideal without recognizing the patriarchal base of the myths he employs. He wishes here to revitalize human sexuality and the sense of awe that certain myths express in the presence of the idealized woman's body. But in so doing he ignores the realities experienced by women in a male-dominated culture. It will be interesting to see in what ways Snyder revises this poem as he works it into the complete version of *Mountains and Rivers,* given his deepening understanding of the interrelationship of ecology and feminism and the necessity of a truly gender-equal society. One also finds here, according to Peter Georgelos, the beginnings of Snyder's cross-fertilization of Shamanism and Buddhism. And Steuding claims that this is a developing tendency in *Mountains and Rivers* as Snyder, upon his 1968 return to the United States, began to see himself more as American shaman than Zen student.[16]

"The Market" records a series of Snyder's reflections made during an experience in India. As the poem's closing lines record, "I came to buy / a few bananas by the ganges / while waiting for my wife" (33). This poem too is set in the city, but it is troubled rather than ecstatic. It expresses doubt about the pervasiveness of "goodwill" in the world and the degree to which commodity fetishism obscures human recognition of the interdependence and co-creativity of the universe. Most of part two of "The Market" consists of a set of equations expressing the varied parities of exchange value around the world and emphasizing the disparity of life. Part three outlines some of the demonic results when exchange value replaces goodwill as the basis for human relationships. But as Snyder indicated to Faas, the reader can only go so far with this poem because it raises a question that Snyder will have to answer in a later part of the sequence: "When you break your customary set of equivalences, then where do you go?"[17]

"Journeys" works a bit like the beginning section of "The Elwha River" in that it utilizes the interpenetration of dream imagery and historical memory. It takes the reader through several worlds both to break down normal channels of rational thought and to tap into the unconscious through archetypes and myths. Part one is another dream sequence in which a bird becomes a woman who then leads the first-person narrator through a subterranean journey. Her gift of a slice of apple awakens him, an obvious parody of the Adam and Eve myth, as well as possibly an allusion to the tale of Sleeping Beauty. Parts two and three, with no apparent indication of being dreams, depict the narrator and others as traveling in a strange land. As primitive hunters they reach a plateau where they flee the sun in awe of its power while shooting arrows at it.

The next two parts seem to be individual recollections of real events, but their relationship to the primitive hunter story remains unclear. Part six heightens whatever confusion the reader may have because it is a journey into the mountains that ends "now I have come to the LOWLANDS" (36). The last three parts of the poem are crucial to unraveling its mysteries and the elliptical relationships among its preceding parts. Part seven returns to the dream format, depicting a scatological urban nightmare. Part eight, in contrast, takes place in the quotidian world, portraying a bus ride. But by now the distinction between dream narratives and this travel narrative has blurred—all are journeys, with the physical and the psychic interpenetrating. In the final section, the narrator is traveling again with a friend. It begins: "We were following a long river into the mountains" (37). The spiritual components presented as early as "Bubbs Creek Haircut" are here: water as energy, mountains as form, and friendship as human interaction. It starts out like the preceding travel narrative, but then:

> Ko grabbed me and pulled me over the cliff—
> both of us falling. I hit and I was dead. I saw
> my body for a while, then it was gone. Ko was
> there too. We were at the bottom of the gorge.
> We started drifting up the canyon, "This is the
> way to the back country." (37)

As in "Bubbs Creek Haircut," a moment of sudden enlightenment is depicted here. The narrator has shed his ego and with it his sense of body as separate from the rest of the world. Object and subject interpenetrate, and as they do each disappears. Snyder probably uses "Ko" for his companion's name since it is the Indo-European root for "together," but it may also be an abbreviation of Ko'kopilau. Snyder may very well also be rehearsing a little myth of the Prajna Paramitra Sutra, the doctrine that form equals emptiness. What is a canyon but an empty form, defined by the space between cliffs? That this sutra is important to the *Mountains and Rivers* sequence is made explicit by Snyder in one of the sections not collected in book form but published the year after *Six Plus One*, "The Hump-backed Flute Player."[18] There Snyder identifies two crucial figures in the sequence: Hsuan Tsang, the Chinese wandering Buddhist who brought this sutra and others from India to China in the seventh century A.D.; and, Ko'kopilau, the Native American mythical humpbacked flute player who carried seeds and warmed the air with his flute in the spring. These two also serve through their similarities to link Buddhism and Native Shamanism.

It is precisely this mixture of Buddhism and Shamanism that constitutes the basis for "The Blue Sky," the additional poem of *Six Plus One.* As Beongchen Yu explains it, in this poem Snyder combines both Hsuan Tsang and Koko'pilau "in the figure of 'Old Man Medicine Buddha,' the archetypal healer, and thereby justifies his personal convictions about the poet's function as a shaman"; and Snyder states that "it's the jump from the healing impulse in Buddhism to a North American shamanistic healing that I'm really trying to get across."[19] Several critics have initiated explications of this, the most allusive and complex section of *Mountains and Rivers* published to date.[20] One, Julia Martin, makes an extremely helpful observation: "The eye is shifted from one fragment to the next, and yet the poem is about making 'whole'? Yes! The poem must foreground this process, because to conceive of 'wholeness' outside the continual play of difference and interdependence, to desire the attainment of a transcendent Absolute . . . is, according to the teaching of sunyata [emptiness], to remain bound by that desire."[21]

What Snyder eventually hopes to accomplish with *Mountains and Rivers,* given its difficulties and complexities and its synthesis of Buddhism and Shamanism, may be suggested by two remarks he has made over the years, one in the mid-1960s and one in the mid-1970s:

We won't be white men a thousand years from now. We won't be white men *fifty* years from now. Our whole culture is going someplace else. The work of poetry is to capture those areas of the consciousness which belong to the American continent, the non-white world.

But the capacity of communication has many levels and the most fundamental in a sense remains the communication of inward states of being.[22]

The Back Country

It can be argued that *The Back Country* is at least as much about that ''communication of inward states of being'' as it is a record of Snyder's experiences in the western United States and Asia. Part of the reason for such a claim rests with the fact that Snyder does not stick to geographic subtitles for the four main sections of this book. They are ''Far West,'' ''Far East,'' ''Kālī,'' and ''Back.'' Although Kālī includes poems from Snyder's visit to India, the majority of them treat memories of Snyder's years in the West and Japan. And ''Back,'' although focusing again on the western United States, may also be read as *back from Kālī*. If one thinks of the archetypal quest motif of separation, initiation, return, with the West being what Snyder separates from in order to experience initiation in Japan while on his quest for Buddhist enlightenment, then the ''Kālī'' section parallels the visit to the underworld that so many epic heroes undertake, including certain Buddhas. And ''Back,'' then, is the return not only to the West but also to the human world and to responsible immersion in human society.

The Back Country has a somewhat complicated history in that it first began coming together in 1966, with an intermediate version appearing in a 1967 limited edition and the final version, with its subtitles and translations of Miyazawa Kenji's poems, appearing in 1968. The 1966 unfinished version included in Snyder's *A Range of Poems* contains approximately half the poems that appear in the 1968 edition. Snyder explained the book in this way to bibliographer Katherine McNeill: ''I arranged it very deliberately, section by section, but it's mixed, a very diverse gathering of poems, and some of them are much better than others.''[23] Part of that diversity reflects the fact that these eighty-six poems, plus eighteen translated poems, were written over a fifteen-year period. The first poem, ''A Berry Feast,'' was written about 1953 and originally intended for inclusion in *Myths & Texts,* but others were written as late as 1966. Some seventeen poems appear in print here for the first time, but clearly most of them were written much earlier (the poems Snyder wrote during the construction of *The Back Country* from 1966 to 1968 are largely reserved for his next volume of poetry, *Regarding Wave*).

What is most interesting about this collection as a book is that Snyder chose it to mark his permanent return to the United States. By that time he had a solid reputation and he was in the process of writing a series of celebratory poems, as well as preparing to publish a significant prose volume, *Earth House Hold.* Yet, instead of preparing a book of triumph, Snyder marked his return to the United States with a book that recorded the difficulties, the failures, and the doubts with which he had been dealing during his extended period of Buddhist study. Proclamations of enlightenment and ecstasy would for the most part have to wait for the record of his marriage to Masa Uehara in *Regarding Wave.*

As Steuding notes, ''the trials and tribulation, the pain and exaltation of [Snyder's] psychic journey, his quest for sanity and wholeness, are recorded'' in *The Back Country.*[24] It is useful to keep in mind that Snyder began to put together the volume following the end of his relationship with Kyger and before he had clearly determined his return to the United States. During this process, also, his roshi (Buddhist master teacher), with whom he had been in daily contact for long periods of time, died. As a result, many of the poems refer to ended relationships and treat family as a crucial dimension of his life to which he hoped to return. From this vantage point, then, the first three sections can be expected to contain grief, nostalgia, self-recrimination, and an emotional range of memories.

"Far West"

"A Berry Feast" appropriately opens "Far West" because it is one of Snyder's very early mature poems. Grounded in Native American cultural beliefs, it emphasizes the survival and carnival trickster life of Coyote. It also sets up a parallel with the poem "Oysters," which closes "Back." Both speak of feasts through immersion and gathering in wild nature. "A Berry Feast," however, emphasizes fecundity and sexuality, both through the mythic Coyote and Bear stories, as well as in the real-life story in the poem about the nursing mother who was part of this berry-picking group. In the same way that Han-shan is used elsewhere, Coyote partly figures here as a stand-in for the Beat generation, the 1950s intentionally vulgar rebellious youth and their hitchhiking, anti-establishment ways:

> —and when Magpie
> Revived him, limp rag of fur in the river
> Drowned and drifting, fish-food in the shallows,
> "Fuck you!" sang Coyote
> and ran.[25]

As indicated in part four of the poem, there is an intense effort to live in the present moment without reason or justification for such a choice; hence the frequent leaps into a type of animal consciousness. At the same time the poem reflects a certain bravado about Snyder's path in life, while it ironically reveals him as the one looking on at the relationship of the Matsons, personal friends to whom the poem is dedicated, and trying to create a sense of self through adoption of another culture's beliefs.

A less ecstatic poem, which depicts Snyder without the cultural trappings of others, and alone amidst nature, is "Six-Month Song in the Foothills." Jody Norton provides the most succinct interpretation of this poem: "These seasonal activities take place in a shared home . . . and in the larger shared home of nature. In their home-in-nature neither being interferes with the other, bird and man pursuing separate works, separate ends without destructiveness or hostility."[26] And Charles Altieri emphasizes the antitranscendental quality of the poem, in many ways in contradiction to some of the yearning felt in "A Berry Feast": "Man does not have to transcend nature; he has only to recognize how that flux generates meaning."[27] Significantly the bird in the poem is a swallow, a migrator, like the birds Snyder identifies with in *Riprap,* who will travel far, only to return. And although the "shed" with which the poem begins and ends is clearly intended in its literal meaning—the place where the action occurs—it can also be associated with the kind of "shedding" of things and ideas that the acolyte of "Bubbs Creek Haircut" undertakes.

Another 1960 poem, "A Walk," returns to the Yosemite riprapping days for its action. This poem is almost entirely stripped of elements that do not contribute to literal depiction of a day's activity. Michael Castro believes that it "works convincingly as a poem because it accurately registers impressions in a language appropriate to their immediacy and in a form that synthesizes the natural rhythms of voice, sense, and the experience in nature that is the poem's subject."[28] But the title seriously understates this little adventure and thereby emphasizes what Altieri sees as the crucial relationship between the difficulty of the trek to Benson Lake and the swim and lunch that Snyder enjoys at journey's end before his return to camp.

But while that tension is important to the plot of the poem, Altieri's reading ignores the extensive set of human-animal-environment relationships that Snyder presents. The first few lines establish a parallel among the mules, Murphy, and Snyder, all of whom are relaxing because it is Sunday. Similarly, once Snyder sets out he is immersed in a heavily populated landscape in which everyone, including him, is on the move, skittering, running, shimmering, wading. Throughout, a sense of mutual respect defines the relationships between the local animals and this visiting human animal. The end of the poem also establishes that Snyder's walk is part of a larger, ongoing and relatively undisturbing human presence, as indicated by the little three-year-old trail-crew cooking stove that he finds at his destination.

But the walk on Sunday cannot be separated from the rhythms of work. "Fire in the Hole" (13) describes the dynamiting part of trail-crew work but tellingly ends with the recognition that the narrators' "hands and arms and shoulders" have been freed. Exertion leads to liberation in this setting, but actually the freedom is relative, a pause before the resumption of labor. Both are part of the rhythm of universal energy transfer, as suggested by the next poem, "Burning the Small Dead" (13). Norton provides a careful structural reading of this poem, emphasizing the way in which the temporal scope of the poem widens out in "quantum leaps" through its five parts.

The line "Burning the small dead" calls forth in the reader's mind a more apocalyptic scenario—such as burning babies or sacrificial animals—than the poem presents in its bonfire of "branches." The power of the poem resides precisely in its ability to be simultaneously metonymic, explicitly literal, and metaphoric, each object a symbol for some dimension of human culture. What is most moving in the poem is the way in which Snyder telescopes out from the fire of the burning branches to the burning stars in the sky and yet imbues each with a sense of temporality. All is process, and all contains the rest. The branches that hiss in the elemental fire consist of the other three classical elements: water, earth, and air. A universe is contained therein, but it is a universe burning, transferring energy across its vast reaches.

Several of the poems that follow could have easily been added to *Riprap,* having been composed at or about the same period of time, but clearly not the closing one of this section. "For the Boy Who Was Dodger Point Lookout Fifteen Years Ago" (31) was not written until 1965. As Snyder indicates in a prefatory note, it is about a backpacking trip he took with his first wife about 1950. As Sherman Paul notes, "the poem is also for the *boy* Snyder was fifteen years ago.''[29] His depiction of Alison as ''Swan Maiden'' clarifies the nostalgic stance of the poem, idealizing her, and idealizing this brief moment of utter tranquility. Snyder expresses a sense of loss and a feeling of self-pity for the way he has perhaps too easily ''shed'' his relationships with others. Being alone in wilderness has its benefits and opportunities for spiritual growth, but standing alone may prove inadequate in the face of a brutal world that Snyder describes as ''muddy,'' ''blood-drenched,'' and filled with lies. The images here prepare the reader for the ''Kālī'' section yet to come.

"Far East"

''Yase: September'' (35), the first poem of ''Far East,'' strongly shifts tone, suggesting overall that the Japan years to be depicted are an overwhelmingly positive experience. This poem and the four that follow reveal a strong sense of dislocation but also a growing feeling of relation and integration. ''Yase'' describes what Snyder learned from his Kyoto landlady who, as she managed to cut weeds and pick flowers simultaneously, taught him about the relationship between work and art. The lesson has to do particularly with a sense of oneness with the work and the ability to find beauty in each particularity. As Yamazato notes, ''the implied admiration for her act arises from his perception that, for her, there exists no separation between aestheticism and daily life and work.''[30]

''Pine River'' (36) and ''Vapor Trails'' (37), which follow ''Yase: September,'' function as polar opposites. The first poem finds Snyder working through the continuities and discontinuities of Japan's past and present, its shift from feudalism to capitalism, and feeling the tranquility arising from the lookout's viewpoint while visiting Matsue castle. But such tranquility is shattered in ''Vapor Trails'' by American jets screaming overhead, reminding him of past wars and ''all future war.'' In ''Pine River'' he could lose himself, but in ''Vapor Trails'' he has to affirm his own existence, and his personal commitment to the Buddhism he was intensively practicing, in the face of young American pilots skilled in the craft of war: "I stumble on the cobble rockpath." Here he must concentrate on finding the design of "two-leaf pine" for the same reason that he called upon the memory of the Dodger Point moment—to grope for sanity amidst the civilized world's madness.

But the differences between that familiar Western landscape and Japan are emphasized by his realizations in "Mt. Hiei" (38). In this poem, he cannot do what he would normally do if he were back home. In recalling what his behavior had been when a lookout—mistaking "Aldebaran / for fire"—he admits that he has confused Japan with someplace else. But as "Out West" (39) warns us, Japan is not even what it once was, much less the idealized dream of a young American. What Snyder has found distressing in the United States threatens to destroy, by means of westernization, all that he hoped to find in Japan. Here the new machinery and "that straw hat shaped like a stetson" and the boy's "blue jeans" represent a far more devastating invasion of traditional culture than the jets overhead in "Vapor Trails."

"The Public Bath" (41–42) shows the poet not only immersed in warm water but also in the daily life of common people, using the pronoun "we." Yet he cannot lose his sense of differential identity; he is not Japanese. Recognition of the racial differences seems mostly a result of curiosity on the part of the "bath-girl." But the history of World War II that separates Snyder and his fellow bathers, gruesomely recalled at poem's end, cannot be so easily dismissed. To reinforce for his readers this historical sense of responsibility, Snyder paired "The Public Bath," originally published in 1963, with another poem first published in 1966, "A Volcano in Kyushu" (43). Yamazato points out that these are from two different periods of Snyder's years in Japan; theme rather than chronology links them. In the second poem, Snyder, on Mount Aso, initially thinks of the history of place and geological time that displays a universal interconnectedness of mountains around the

Understanding Gary Snyder

world. But an individual's appearance, "a noseless, shiny, / mouth-twisted middle aged man," interrupts this universalizing nostalgia and shifts Snyder's attention to a more immediate and particular memory: "J. Robert Oppenheimer: / twenty years ago / watching the bulldozers / tearing down pines / at Los Alamos." Nagasaki, one of the two atom bomb targets in World War II, is on Kyushu. The man, like the pines, is a victim of America's destructive might. The Japanese appreciate the "bare rock" created by volcanic power; but the "bare rock" that Oppenheimer helped create can only be abhorred.

Memories of the United States remained strong apparently throughout at least Snyder's first few stays in Japan, as suggested by "Four Poems for Robin" (47–49). The first poem combines the memory of a backpacking trip during which he remembered an undergraduate relationship he had—before he married Alison Gass— with his life now in Japan. It may be the case that Robin here is a composite portrait of this college girlfriend, as well as Alison and, by this time, Joanne, and perhaps others. What comes through is not his desire for a particular life-style but his sense of loneliness when he is not in an emotionally intense sexual relationship. This theme is reiterated in the second poem, most specifically when he claims he has forgotten everything he "wanted then" but her. A ghostly vision of Robin has appeared to Snyder while in Kyoto, significantly in the spring, but his describing it by means of an episode from the well-known Japanese tale of Genji shows Snyder identifying himself more strongly with Japan than with the Pacific Northwest of the first poem.

By autumn in the third poem, this ghostly apparition has become more fierce and bitter. Snyder's remark that he awakened ashamed and angry, remembering "The pointless wars of the heart" (48), suggests that he is perhaps learning the lesson of his nightmare in terms of his own limitations as a partner. He does not speak this time of her body, but only of their hearts. And by December, Snyder has worked through the nightmares and come to some understanding of what has driven these two "star-crossed" lovers apart forever. According to Yamazato, the plan with which Snyder says he is obsessed is to build a Buddhist meditation hall in the United States. And such a plan, in his own mind, meant he must "make it alone," for at least part of his quest for Buddhist wisdom. At the poem's end Snyder knows what he has accomplished, but remains unsure if he has chosen wisely.

But he must move on, and "Six Years" (54–69), the thirteen-section poem that closes "Far East," records his movement through the Japan years up through 1964. "January" establishes a setting and a tone through the depiction of a balanced Japanese landscape. "February" then places him in that landscape, at work cleaning his house. Yamazato notes an important distinction about the use of Japanese words in this poem as compared to others. Here they name aspects of a normal household and everyday life rather than being allusions to Buddhist mythology and literature. As such they demonstrate Snyder's "record of actually trying to enter into the whole taste and flavor of the country and culture."[31] A curious moment occurs, though, in the midst of his meticulous labor, when after observing that "all the different animals are persons," he asks, "what will I do about *Liberation*" (55). In an interview, Snyder explained this kind of descriptive poem by saying that "if I am sweeping the floor and thinking about sweeping the floor, I am all one."[32] Apparently here, his oneness is momentarily interrupted by his compassion for other creatures. But the stray metaphysical question, as in meditation, arises and floats free rather than being latched onto by the conscious mind. In a sense, the close of the poem serves as a koan, with the answer to the question about liberation being "charcoal. black. the fire part red / the ash pure white" (55).

"March" and "April" record two very different experiences of community eating and entertaining and show Snyder alive and immersed in both secular Japanese company and Buddhist monastic company. But in both cases, Snyder identifies and associates with the lowly and the common, not the elite, whether intellectuals or priests. "May" takes him out to the Japanese countryside where he works through a series of associations between Japan and the American Northwest. In contrast, "June" records Snyder's brief experience in 1961 of having to teach English as a second language after he left the Zen institute. Clearly he was not pleased and found himself easily distracted by the mechanical nature of such instruction. And against this he contrasts in "July" a trip to the beach and his observations of the relaxed behavior of the people there. "August" goes a step further, with Snyder recounting an experience of sharing in the labors of a fishing village one evening. And in "September" he records one of the many trips he and Kyger took, but in this one they follow Japanese tradition by staying at an inn.

The tension felt at the beginning of the section regarding Snyder's differences due to race and history have completely fallen away to the point where Snyder can feel comfortable being simply silly in the pronouncements and sloganeering of "October." "November" and "December" place him back at temple work and engaging in the eight-day December Sesshin, an intensive meditation session. The key idea here is that of "a far bell / coming closer," which introduces and ends the poem. At the literal level, this describes the practice during sesshin of awakening the participants at 3:30 A.M. by having a monk run toward the zendo ringing a handheld bell. This image can also be interpreted as Snyder deepening his understanding of Buddhism. Yamazato believes that this poem is based primarily on Snyder's first experience of such a sesshin in 1960. But the placement of the poem in the volume also allows the "far bell" to serve as an image of Snyder readying himself to return to the United States. The "Envoy to Six Years" places Snyder aboard ship, once again heading for the United States. The last line, with him in the bowels of the ship, allies this "envoy" with other engine-room poems that identify work in the engine room as a descent to the underworld.

"Kālī"

The first two poems of "Kālī" are "Alysoun" and "To Hell with Your Fertility Cult" (73). The first line of "Alysoun, "My mother called you Robin," has caused some critics to think that Robin and Alison Gass (Alysoun being assumed an alternate spelling of her name), Snyder's first wife, are the same person. They are not. This line pertains to mistaken identity, which may arise not only from an individual's confusion but also from a split between the conscious and the unconscious as symbolized by the character Alysoun's "evil dreams." Their camping takes place "by dark," so that the experience fits symbolically into the quest motif of "Kālī" as descent to the underworld. Just as the back country can be understood as both wilderness and the positive dimensions of the human unconscious, so too "by dark" can be understood as both night and the negative side of the unconscious.

In "To Hell with Your Fertility Cult," Snyder assumes the viewpoint of the woman, who pelts the male character with a fertilized egg, while the "your" and "he" of the poem could very well be Snyder himself. In this way, by letting the woman speak from her point of view, Snyder is able to atone for his error of objectifying the woman without making himself the focus of the poem. At the same time, the title alludes implicitly to Kālī, who is, among other things, the goddess of fertility and death. Both dimensions of Kālī are represented here by means of the "half-formed chick" whose life has been ended by the woman's violent reaction against any kind of belief that reduces women to objects of appropriation by men.

For Snyder, India was enormously instructive and the lessons painful as well as delightful. The poems published over a ten-year period that Snyder selects for inclusion here tend to record more pain than delight. The time span is important for realizing that the "Kālī" section cannot be read solely as Snyder's reaction to India. Rather, India made him conscious of certain aspects of his own life and mind that he had not previously recognized. It also seems that

Snyder made some significant discoveries about relationships during the two years that he put together *The Back Country*. But Snyder does not allow reflections on his personal relationships to overwhelm this section or to be isolated from the rest of humanity's problems of being in the world. After nine poems, seven of which focus on relationships, Snyder places "This Tokyo" (80–81), originally written in December, 1956. Here Snyder views the entire world as burning with the flames of negative, destructive desires. One of his most pessimistic poems, it perhaps reflects a bitter response to a recognition that he had idealized Japan and Buddhism while he was in the United States. This is certainly no liberating recognition of the void, of the impermanence of material forms. Rather, it is a pessimistic appraisal of the possibilities for the kind of change that he hoped an American Buddhism could bring about in the world.

"The Manichaeans" (82–83), which is dedicated to Kyger, serves as a counterpoint both to the earlier poems about relationships and to the despair of "This Tokyo." But an element of desperation appears here as well insofar as love seems not to exist as an act of fulfillment in and of itself. Rather, the lovers need it to "keep back the cold" of India and of death. The title names a sect that epitomizes the extreme dualistic thinking against which the anti-dualistic act of passionate embracing to create warmth is designed to respond. But the tone remains uncertain, as if the energies of death remain stronger here than those of life. It would seem that overall such is the case throughout the India poems, as exemplified in "Circumambulating Arunachala" (96). Here the vibrancy of life that flower-carrying little girls represent is muffled by the knowledge that "they die or sicken in a year." From a Buddhist standpoint, Snyder's emphasis rests on the recognition of suffering as a given in the world—part of the going around in circles—rather than on the compassion that can ameliorate it. Snyder does not accept this dying as simply part of the impermanence of the world but feels that modern society has exacerbated such suffering.

Despite the recordings of pessimism, despair, doubt, rejection, and failure, Snyder does not end "Kālī" on any of these notes. "Go Round" (105) presents a Zen resolution of the contradictions of India by seeing them as part of the wheel of life, death, and rebirth, which need not simply be a "go-round"—a circumambulation—but can be experienced as a "*merry*-go-round" (my emphasis). Here Snyder focuses on the Zen emphasis on the present moment in contrast to the Hindu emphasis on teleology and the end goal of escaping rebirth. The last poem of "Kālī," "[After Rāmprasād Sen]" (106), reinforces this stance by presenting rebirth as a positive rather than negative event. It may indicate inadequacies of a past life or the failures of one's own earlier life, but rebirth opens up again the opportunity to "dance."

"Back"

Charles Molesworth concludes that " 'Back' resolves the negative tones that threaten to dominate all of the volume and does so by turning to figures of sensual completion and harmony, for which the epitome is the figure of graceful movement or dance,"[33] which is prefigured in the last poem of "Kālī." "For the West" (115–17) uses the imagery of women, from Europa through white American women to a "little girl," to suggest that some deeper fundamental activity of procreativity and movement charts the future for humanity in contrast to the technology and consumerism that seem to drive the Western world. Europe and the United States in their present form are an aberration, a "flowery glistening oil blossom," but one fated to disappear so that the poet can "see down again through clear water." Nothing has been resolved, the United States has not yet changed, but the poet now has the vision to see beneath the appearances to the fluid magma under the crust of Pax Americana. And what he realizes is that change is so dynamic and far-reaching that it can never be intellectually measured, plotted, and predicted. As he realizes in "Twelve Hours out of New York After Twenty-Five Days at Sea" (119), "I did not mean to come this far." Even an individual life surpasses any rational plan, just as gardens change with the seasons.

In order to perceive that change and flow, a person has to rely on intuition and sensation: "What 'is' within not known" ("Beneath My Hand and Eye the Distant Hills, Your Body," 123). But such intuition cannot be simply attained. "Through the Smoke Hole" indicates that it comes through cultivating deep cultural and spiritual practices, such as that of the kiva rituals practiced by Southwestern Indians, beginning with the Hohokam precursors of the Anasazi and Hopi. But the kiva is a model only for emulation.[34] The concluding point, that "plain men / come out of the ground" (127), emphasizes humanity's origin as well as its ongoing relationship with the earth. To be able to affirm rebirth and societal vision one must be grounded, physically and culturally, in place and practice. And despite whatever Japanese Buddhism would have to offer the United States, the cultural practices already in place here for thousands of years will also have to be taken into account, learned from, and brought forward. It is also fitting that the "smoke hole" imagery is employed here, toward the end of *The Back Country,* because it clearly signals that the poet has safely returned from a psychic/spiritual underworld.

The Back Country four-part series of poems ends with a deceptively simple poem, "Oysters" (128). The key line, repeated and emphasized by Snyder, is "ALL WE WANTED," but what exactly constitutes "all" remains more implied than stated. For the characters in the poem it means feeding on the wild natural plenitude the planet has available for human habitation. Altieri draws this conclusion about the poem: "Only when one learns to control the desire for plenitude by a sense of the simple necessities whose satisfaction constitutes one mode of that plenitude will one free the dream and the dreamer from the bitter disillusionment that often torments self-consciousness."[35] In terms of the volume as a whole, then, Snyder has freed himself from certain expectations and idealizations of Japan and Buddhism, fears and repressions of his own unconscious, and recriminations about his own past failures, particularly in relationships. And he has done so, like the acolyte in "Bubbs Creek Haircut," by going through these experiences and stages of awareness rather than withdrawing from them. The volume ends, then, with a tone of tranquility and peace, as well as a sense of place in the larger flux of universal energy exchange.

"Miyazawa Kenji"

Appended to *The Back Country* are Snyder's translations of the poems by Miyazawa Kenji. One can see affinities between Snyder's poetry and these poems, which Hisao Kanaseki has clearly outlined.[36] But they do not add to an understanding of Snyder or his poetics. They are not part of the British edition of *The Back Country,* since they had already appeared in *A Range of Poems* the year before. When New Directions published its edition, this section was added because the poems had not yet appeared in the United States.

Even without the translations, *The Back Country* is a large collection and one of uneven quality. In the early 1970s, fellow poet Alan Williamson paid respectful tribute to Snyder, commenting that his short poems seemed "subtler" and "more intellectually suggestive" than those of his contemporaries. And as for the more ambitious poems of *The Back Country*, Williamson claims that they are "remarkable alike for their historical insight and for the canny humor and daring that spring from Snyder's essential mystic's disbelief in history."[37]

Notes

1. Gary Snyder, *Six Sections from Mountains and Rivers without End Plus One* (1970; rpt. Bolinas, Ca.: Four Seasons Foundations, 1979). Hereafter cited in the text as *Six Plus One*.

Understanding Gary Snyder

2. James W. Kraus, "Appendix A, Interview I: June 15, 1983," in "Gary Snyder's Biopoetics: A Study of the Poet as Ecologist," Ph.D. dissertation, University of Hawaii, 1986, 181–82.

3. Dave Robertson, "Practicing the Wild—Present and Future Plans: An Interview with Gary Snyder," in *Critical Essays on Gary Snyder,* ed. Patrick D. Murphy (Boston: G. K. Hall, 1990) 259.

4. Peter Georgelos has noted, in "Post-structural 'Traces' in the Work of Gary Snyder" (M.A. thesis, University of Western Ontario, 1987) 53, that "one could say that the poems will eventually 'feed off' of each other as if the book were a linguistic food web. But until this is accomplished some of the sections already published appear to be quite difficult and incomplete."

5. Snyder quoted by Ekbert Faas, "Gary Snyder," in *Towards A New American Poetics: Essays & Interviews* (Santa Barbara: Black Sparrow Press, 1979) 132.

6. "*Noh,* a medieval play with dancing and recitation much influenced by Buddhism, is one of the most important Japanese literary elements of influence on Snyder's poetry," according to Katsunori Yamazato, "Seeking a Fulcrum: Gary Snyder and Japan (1956–1975)," Ph.D. dissertation, University of California, Davis, 1987, 61.

7. Bob Steuding, *Gary Snyder* (Boston: Twayne, 1976) 95–96.

8. For a discussion of this poem and "Journeys" as mythic fantasy poems, see my essay "Mythic and Fantastic: Gary Snyder's 'Mountains and Rivers without End,' " *Extrapolation* 26 (1985) 290–99. Part of the interpretation here is based on that essay.

9. The head-shaving and its significance is explained by Anthony Hunt in " 'Bubbs Creek Haircut': Gary Snyder's 'Great Departure' in *Mountains and Rivers without End,*" *Western American Literature* 15 (1980) 167–69. My interpretation of this poem is heavily indebted to Hunt's essay.

10. Hunt 169–71.

11. Tantra is "a pan-Indian religious form involving magical ritual, depending on a guru, and sometimes sexual practices," according to Robert Aitken, *The Mind of Clover: Essays in Zen Buddhist Ethics* (San Francisco: North Point Press, 1984) 199. For Snyder, the sexual practices were a significant dimension.

12. Faas 135. Snyder refers to this as Avatamsaka, or "Flower Wreath" Buddhism, which in China is known as Hua-Yen and in Japan as Kegon.

13. See Georgelos 41–42 for this story and its relevance to Snyder's thought.

14. Yamazato 89.

15. Yamazato 63.

16. Steuding 93.

17. Faas 137.

18. Gary Snyder, "The Hump-backed Flute Player," *Coyote's Journal* #9 (1971) 1–4.

19. Beongchen Yu, *The Great Circle: American Writers and the Orient* (Detroit: Wayne State University Press, 1983) 223; Steuding may very well be the

Of Mountains, Rivers, and Back Country

source for Yu's observation. Snyder has also remarked that "this poem is based on the sutra of the Buddha of healing, Bhaishajyaguru, otherwise known as Yakushi" (Katherine McNeill, *Gary Snyder: A Bibliography* [New York: Phoenix Bookshop, 1983] 53).

20. See Steuding 105–109.

21. Julia Martin, "Writing the Wild: Sunyata in Gary Snyder's Ecological Politics," *Proceedings of the Fu Jen University, Taiwan, Second International Conference on Literature and Religion,* forthcoming.

22. Steuding (102) quotes the first passage from a TV interview: "Philip Whalen and Gary Snyder," *Poetry U.S.A.* (Bloomington, Indiana, National Educational Television interview, 1965); the second passage comes from Faas (138).

23. McNeill 35.

24. Steuding 122

25. Gary Snyder, *The Back Country* (New York: New Directions, 1968, 1971) 5. Subsequent page references will be given in the text.

26. Jody Norton, "The Importance of Nothing: Absence and Its Origins in the Poetry of Gary Snyder," *Contemporary Literature* 28 (1987); rpt. in Murphy 180.

27. Charles Altieri, *Enlarging the Temple: New Directions in American Poetry during the 1960's* (Lewisburg, Pa.: Bucknell University Press, 1979) 137.

28. Michael Castro, "Gary Snyder: The Lessons of *Turtle Island,*" in *Interpreting the Indian: Twentieth-Century Poets and the American Indian* (Albuquerque: University of New Mexico Press, 1984); rpt. in *Critical Essays on Gary Snyder,* ed. Patrick D. Murphy (Boston: G. K. Hall, 1990) 133.

29. Sherman Paul, *In Search of the Primitive: Rereading David Antin, Jerome Rothenberg, and Gary Snyder* (Baton Rouge: Louisiana State University Press, 1986) 253.

30. Yamazato 76.

31. Yamazato 75, 80.

32. Gary Snyder, *The Real Work: Interviews & Talks 1964–1979,* ed. Wm. Scott McLean (New York: New Directions, 1980) 7.

33. Charles Molesworth, *Gary Snyder's Vision: Poetry and the Real Work* (Columbia: University of Missouri Press, 1983) 52.

34. See Castro 142.

35. Altieri 143.

36. Hisao Kanaseki, "An Easy Rider at Yase," in *Gary Snyder: Dimensions of a Life,* ed. Jon Halper (San Francisco: Sierra Club Books, 1991) 73–74.

37. Alan Williamson, "Language Against Itself: The Middle Generation of Contemporary Poets," in *American Poetry Since 1960—Some Critical Perspectives,* ed. Robert B. Shaw (Cheshire, U.K.: Carcanet Press, 1973) 62.

CHAPTER FIVE

The Waves of Household and Marriage: *Earth House Hold* and *Regarding Wave*

Earth House Hold

Snyder's first published prose volume, *Earth House Hold: Technical Notes & Queries to Fellow Dharma Revolutionaries* (1969), is similar to *The Back Country* in that it collects pieces written and published over a sixteen-year period, 1952–1968. At first glance it may seem a miscellany, consisting of a mixture of journals, reviews, translations, and essays. Snyder did, however, carefully select the materials, omitting some prose pieces and arranging items in roughly chronological order. As he explains it, "the way of putting all the pieces in *Earth House Hold* together is in a sense a poetic rather than a prosodic composition, in an essentially field perception manner. . . . they are miscellaneous, but they touch base with a lot of what I think are important points of my own education."[1]

There are two fundamentally different, even though complementary, ways to read this volume: one, the most common, to use it as a reference work to interpret the poetry, particularly in order to emphasize the autobiographical dimensions of the verse; two, to read it as a work standing on its own, designed to educate people in the United States at a particular moment in history. *Earth House Hold* can be profitably read as a reference work alongside of virtually any of Snyder's poetry written up through 1968. Readers who take this approach, however, tend to overlook the book's integrity as an aesthetic artifact, often ignoring its own internal structures and resonances. They also tend to forget that, when it was published in a first printing of ten thousand copies, many people read the book without having read any of Snyder's other work and so were not comparing it with his poems or reading it to learn about those poems. As the subtitle suggests, the book was oriented toward a specific audience in the United States. Such "Dharma revolutionaries" would be reading *Earth House Hold* to see what Snyder had to say about ecological change, spiritual transformation, and social revolution.

The Back Country outlines a circular journey that takes Snyder from the western United States to Japan and then India and back to the West. *Earth House Hold* brings the reader forward in time to Snyder's marriage to Masa Uehara. His permanent return to the back country of the western United States is here firmly anchored in ecological practice and the responsibilities of marriage and householding. Much of the volume comprises a primer on Snyder's own spiritual education; it also contains his positions on the direction for ecological and spiritual practice in the United States at the beginning of the 1970s.

Many of the entries teach by example, with this method reinforced particularly by Snyder's "Record of the Life of the Ch'an Master Po-chang Huai-Hai." Translated without commentary, this essay provides an argument about the need for discipline, for training, and for a specific spiritual practice: Ch'an Buddhism, called Zen in Japan (Po-chang lived prior to the division of Ch'an [Zen] into two major schools: Ts'ao T'ung [Soto] and Lin-chi [Rinzai]). Most significant here is the final section, "The Regulations of the Ch'an Line," emphasizing discipline, community, and comradeship. Such practices are necessary to insure the flourishing of the Dharma and the transmission of the "three inheritances": "if the three inheritances (word, deed, and thought) are not good, men cannot live together."[2] As Snyder remarked in a 1985 interview, "Buddhism is not just a religion or practice of personal, psychological self-knowledge and enlightenment, but is also a practice of actualizing personal insights in the real world."[3]

The five items included in *Earth House Hold* that precede the Po-chang translation cover the years 1952–1958, roughly the same period treated in *Riprap*. The first entry, "Lookout's Journal," records Snyder's work in the summers of 1952 and 1953 on Crater Mountain and Sourdough Mountain respectively. Sherman Paul's long essay, "From Lookout to Ashram," devotes considerable attention to "Lookout's Journal," comparing it favorably with Thoreau's *Walden*. According to Paul, "changing one's point of view (adjusting the mechanism of perception) is the revolutionary issue; only a discipline as radical as that undertaken by Snyder will, he believes, create an ecological conscience."[4] The second item consists of two 1954 reviews of *Indian Legends of the Pacific Northwest* and *Indian Tales*. By including them Snyder emphasizes that his education comes from Native American as well as Asian sources.

The third entry is from journals kept during his first trip to Japan in 1957–58. Although generally less intense, more descriptive, and far more sketchy than "Lookout's Journal," "Japan First Time Around" records realizations significant for the poet's intellectual development. Snyder's recognitions, for instance, of the connections among Zen, Avatamsaka, and Tantra suggest the need for people to develop a syncretic rather than dogmatic or separatist spiritual path in the present (34). This syncretism will be reflected in his own practice more than twenty years later in the United States in setting up the Ring of Bone Zendo in California. Further, Snyder recognizes, and promotes, affiliations between Zen and "the subtle steady single-beat of oldest American-Asian shamanism" (35). And perhaps his best-known statement from this journal: "Comes a time when the poet must choose: either to step deep in the stream of his people, history, tradition, folding and folding himself in wealth of persons and pasts; philosophy, humanity, to become richly foundationed and great and sane and ordered. Or, to step beyond the bound onto the way out, into horrors and angels . . . possible enlightened return, possible ignominious wormish perishing'' (39).

"Spring Sesshin at Shokoku-Ji" records Snyder's experience of intensive Zen practice. Whereas the Japan journals present what Snyder thought about his Buddhist studies and experience of living in Japan, this passage describes his actual practice during one of the annual intensive meditation periods at the temple compound. "Tanker Notes" follows with another kind of practice, that of being a seaman working his way from Japan back to the United States via the Middle East and the South Pacific. The Po-chang translation is followed by a brief excerpt describing the early 1960s trip with Joanne Kyger to India.

Having established the authority to speak through the presentation of his personal practice in these formative years and the spiritual traditions in which that practice is taking place, Snyder then focuses on his perceptions of the implementation of such practice in North America in the mid-1960s. He does this with "Buddhism and the Coming Revolution" (written in 1961, revised 1967), "Passage to More than India," "Why Tribe," "Poetry and the Primitive," and "Dharma Queries" (all written in 1967), interrupted by a 1965 journal of a summer in the mountains, reminding readers of Snyder's continuous grounding in wilderness. Throughout these essays, Snyder intimately connects ecological activism and Buddhism. For example, he writes: "The soil, the forests and all animal life are being consumed by these cancerous collectivities. . . . The joyous and voluntary poverty of Buddhism becomes a positive force. The traditional harmlessness and refusal to take life in any form has nation-shaking implications" (91).

Perhaps most to the point in terms of Snyder's own practice are his relatively newfound emphases on "tribe" and "family," both of which elaborate on his general remarks about "community."

Snyder is not satisfied merely with a negative critique of America's ills but sees as well the need to offer alternatives. "We use the term Tribe," he writes, "because it suggests the type of new society now emerging within the industrial nations" (113). In a 1977 interview, Snyder remarked that "the natural unit of practice is the family. The natural unit of the play of practice is the community."[5] Interestingly enough, Snyder ends the collection with another illustration of practice. "Suwa-no-se Island and the Banyan Ashram" describes Snyder and Masa Uehara's wedding and concludes on an optimistic note, appropriate for newlyweds, and consonant with the general attitude of those in the United States at the end of the 1960s that revolution was in the air and a new culture on the verge of being born.

Regarding Wave

Given the tremendously optimistic conclusion to *Earth House Hold,* it comes as little surprise that within two months of its appearance Snyder published an extremely celebratory collection of poems and songs. *Regarding Wave* was initially published in a limited edition by Windhover Press of Iowa City in conjunction with a poetry reading given at the University of Iowa.[6] Sixteen months later New Directions brought out an enlarged edition of *Regarding Wave.*[7] The first three parts, "Regarding Wave I," "Regarding Wave II," and "Regarding Wave III," are identical to the text of the Windhover edition. To these, Snyder added two sections: "Long Hair," containing twenty-one poems, and "Target Practice," comprising fifteen mostly brief and playful poems.

"Regarding Wave I"
The celebration of *Regarding Wave* never becomes escape from reality. Instead, it often serves to widen radically reader perception of what should be recognized as real. Such is the case in the col-

lection's second poem, "Seed Pods," an ecstatic meditation that connects the poet's own experience of sexual intercourse with a variety of other transmissions of life-building matter, such as the seeds "caught and carried in the fur" (4). "By the Tama River at the North End of the Plain in April" (7) situates Gary and Masa as lovers within a human community in the larger natural community. Steuding sums it up in this way: "In *Regarding Wave,* energy manifestations—or fields such as mind (consciousness), language (voice), and food (meat and plants)—combine and are given expression in terms of Snyder's domestic situation that is made symbolic."[8] But not all is celebration. The last two poems of "Regarding Wave I" speak of the Vietnam war and its life-destroying effects. Contrasting with the previous poems celebrating life-affirming fertility and sexual activity, "In the House of the Rising Sun" emphasizes "burned-off jungles" and "new Asian strains of clap" (9). And "White Devils" depicts American urbanization's rape of nature, vividly imaged by a still-living, gutted wolf (10). Snyder presents here Buddhist recognitions that suffering is a given in the world and that compassion is the proper response to such suffering.

These are not the poems, however, that have attracted the most attention in "Regarding Wave I." "Wave," the opening poem, has received as much commentary as any other in the entire volume. And critics often turn to Snyder himself for assistance in interpretation, citing a brief section of "Poetry and the Primitive" in *Earth House Hold* subtitled "The Voice as a Girl" (123–26). There Snyder theorizes that "Poetry is voice, and according to Indian tradition, voice, vak (vox)—is a Goddess. Vāk is also called Sarasvati. . . . As Vāk is wife to Brahma ('wife' means 'wave' means 'vibrator' in Indo-European etymology) so the voice, in everyone, is a mirror of his own deepest self. The voice rises to meet an inner need" (124–25). The poem "Wave" (3), then, is about the woman to whom the volume is dedicated: Masa. She is the "wave" who answers Snyder's "inner need."

Some critics believe that the first stanza treats ''disparate objects,'' but actually these are related. On one level, as Bert Almon notes, ''Physics and Mahayana Buddhism would agree that there are no stable objects, merely the illusion of stability.''[9] Snyder observes in ''The Voice as a Girl'' that ''the conch shell is an ancient symbol of the sense of hearing, and of the female; the vulva and the fruitful womb'' (125). The waves of the clam shell are reflected in the striations of rock, trees, sand dunes, and lava flows. Both inorganic and organic manifestations of the non-human form part of the earth, which is mythically rendered as Gaia, the Earth Mother. Since Snyder himself tends to conceptualize the Earth as female and to associate fertility with both women and nature, it comes as no surprise that Masa can take on in his imagination all of these manifestations of the cosmic and the sacred, while remaining physical and sensual.

It is important not to forget that this and other poems in the three sections of ''Regarding Wave'' are not only metaphorical but also metonymic, not just symbolic but also literal. At least in part this poem, as well as the one that concludes ''Regarding Wave III,'' is about a real person inspiring Snyder's life to the point that he images her as a goddess. ''Wave'' is not jut a metaphor for relationships but also narrates the story of energy transfers throughout the universe. The phrase in the poem ''every grain a wave'' accurately depicts the wave/particle relationship of matter, as well as images a Buddhist conception of human life as a particular turbulence in the energy flow. Voice is wave produced by vibrations. Love is also a wave produced by the couple's shared psychic and physical vibrations.

''Regarding Wave II''

''Regarding Wave II'' comprises seven poems. In March 1968 in *Poetry* magazine, Snyder published six of these along with ''Wave'' at the end and ''The Rabbit'' at the beginning as ''Eight

Songs of Clouds and Water." Steuding believes that "The Rabbit" will eventually appear in *Mountains and Rivers without End,* and so it was not reprinted in *Regarding Wave.* Snyder places at the end here a poem not previously published, "Archaic Round and Keyhole Tombs." This arrangement of poems suggests that it makes sense to read "Regarding Wave II" as a set following "Wave." There may very well be a rather elaborate pun involved with the "Clouds and Water" title in that the Zen term for a monk is "unsui," although one would not know this from the book version alone.

In a footnote in *Earth House Hold,* Snyder states that "the term is literally 'cloud, water'—taken from a line of an old Chinese poem, 'To drift like clouds and flow like water.' . . . One takes no formal vows upon becoming an Unsui. . . . After becoming temple priests . . . the great majority of Zen monks marry and raise families" (44). One can easily see here the relationship between the literal meaning of "unsui" and the imagery of "Wave," as well as the relationship of the poems to the phases of Snyder's own life.

In "Song of the Cloud" (13), while emphasizing the drifting movement of clouds, Snyder also alludes to temple life in terms of the activity of sweeping. In the second stanza, the breakdown between subject and object, human and nonhuman, becomes more explicit as the speaker identifies himself as a cloud. Snyder also approvingly notes the ecological diversity of cloud formations. In the closing lines, he may very well be alluding to the kind of "moving elsewhere" described above, that is, monks marrying and raising families, undertaking a new phase of spiritual practice. Such practice, however, moves one closer to Tantra than to Zen, as suggested by "Song of the Tangle" (14) and its explicit sexuality. Specifically, Snyder seems to be depicting an act of "yab-yum," a Tibetan form of coitus-meditation. Steuding believes that this poem depicts Gary and Masa engaging in such a ritual at a Japanese shrine.[10]

"Song of the Slip" (15) continues this sexual imagery but moves from the particular to the general and shifts from cloud to water imagery. The poem ends on an obvious pun, with such word play continuing in "Song of the View" (16). These two poems could be understood as songs to celebrate the event described in "Song of the Tangle," continuing the emphasis on coitus as sacramental. "Song of the Taste" (17), however, moves beyond this human emphasis, placing sexuality in the context of all natural fertility and the interrelatedness of food chains. Snyder has commented in some detail about this poem: "If you think of eating and killing plants or animals to eat as an unfortunate quirk in the nature of the universe, then you cut yourself off from connecting with the sacramental energy-exchange, evolutionary mutual-sharing aspect of life. And if we talk about evolution of consciousness, we also have to talk about evolution of bodies, which takes place by that sharing of energies . . . which is done by literally eating each other. And that's what communion is."[11]

"Kyoto Born in Spring Song" (18–19) moves to the results of the sexuality already celebrated and the other side of the process of eating each other, which is producing each other, giving birth. Katsunori Yamazato points out that, just as in the previous poem, Snyder erases the "differentiating line" between human and animal by calling all of the offspring "children" and "babies." This erasure is underlined by Snyder's use of several Japanese folktales, which tell stories of human children being born of a melon, a bamboo, a plum, and a bird.[12] Snyder ends by universalizing the primal character of such nondifferentiation. The final poem of "Regarding Wave II" seems to suggest that Snyder views his songs as part of a representation of an archetypal awareness beneath and beyond consciousness. The shape of the tombs identified in the title "Archaic Round and Keyhole Tombs" (20), but which are nowhere mentioned in the poem, represent the efforts of many cultures to depict the tomb as also the womb. The poem fits with the basic imagery of the set, with water represented by the pond and clouds figured by the final line, "Coast out of sight," which parallels the phrase in the first poem of the set, "moving elsewhere."

"Regarding Wave III"

"Regarding Wave III" takes the couple from marriage through the conception and birth of their first child and on to the continuation of their relationship after that event, realizing the promise of "Wave" with reflection and meditation—the "Regarding" component—as well as continued ecstasy. David Robbins has provided an excellent reading of Snyder's epithalamion, or marriage poem, "Burning Island" (23–24).[13] Robbins makes the overall point that "the great action behind the island cycle is the ancient ritual of marriage as a cosmogonic event, signifying creation's renewal" (92). And he goes on to point out that "the poem's surface is thus a field of shifting tones and references without a governing perspective. . . . Students who have difficulty with this poem, I've found, collide instructively with this feature of it" (92). Snyder works to break down the normal distinction between subject and object. The speaker is not seeking to observe but to participate in the cosmic communion of which the sacrament of marriage is but one component. Again, to quote Robbins: "the personal request," which is to "All / Gods" to bless the marriage, "has had to wait upon the larger quest, not only because of the diplomacy of ritual supplication but because the prayer for marital blessing must emerge from a balanced, living relation to the surrounding world if it is to be effective" (104).

And one can see this quest for balance working throughout the poem, as Snyder addresses the gods of the four elements: water ("Wave God"), fire ("Volcano Belly Keeper"), air ("Sky Gods"), and earth ("Earth Mother"). In keeping with the heterosexuality of the marriage, Snyder images the first three sets of gods as male and the final one as female. Balance is also represented through interpenetration, such as the liquid lava being solidified by the water and the creation of the land providing a home for the fish. To some extent Snyder maintains this emphasis on balance, in particular between the cosmic and the specific and between the ecstatic and the mundane throughout "Regarding Wave III." After the ecstatic, richly allusive, aesthetically complex "Burning Island," Snyder places "Roots" (25), a very simple yet subtle poem with obvious symbolism. Then he presents the reader with "Rainbow Body" (26–27), a poem stylistically midway between the previous two. It has the literary complexity of "Burning Island" but limits the language to literal, factual descriptions rather than mythic, symbolic ones. Yet the ecstatic and the spiritual hover in the background, implied through such phrasing as "great drone" and "dazzled ears." The balance of this poem arises from the nondifferentiation of various states of being. As Tom Lavazzi reads it, "the entire poem performs like a living, breathing organism."[14]

The four selections that precede the poem "Regarding Wave" focus on Masa's pregnancy and her giving birth to Kai. "It Was When" (30–31) speculates on the moment of conception. The most important line is "new power in your breath called its place." Here, Snyder attributes the mystery and vitality of voice as arising within Masa, within the woman. Previously he had emphasized such power in relation to his own inspiration, to the role of the poet. But as implied in the final lines of "Wave," he recognizes here that creative inspiration co-originates in male and female, spiritual birth and physical birth.

"The Bed in the Sky" (32) finds Snyder focusing on himself in terms of his changing responsibilities and behaviors in relation to the event celebrated in "It Was When." Yamazato argues that "this is a crucial moment in which the poet emerges out of the world of *The Back Country,* a world permeated, as in Snyder's quotation from Bashō on the dedication page, with wandering spirit."[15] As Yamazato notes, two lines near the end of the poem about the desire to remain alone at night outdoors echo a haiku by Bashō in which the poet does stay out all night. But Snyder says "ought" and does the opposite. He surrenders the fleeting desire of his younger "wandering spirit" and accepts the warmth, companionship, and pleasure, as well as responsibilities, of marriage.

"Kai, Today" (33), the next poem, presents this marriage as if it were fated, through recalling a series of Snyder's and Masa's memories of events that led them to each other. (This poem provides a stunning contrast to "Logging 15" of *Myths & Texts*, in which the speaker recalls a sterile relationship as he fatalistically prepares for the apocalypse at the end of the kalpa cycle.) As for "Not Leaving the House" (34), Steuding observes that "in this poem we can clearly see that Snyder, too, is reborn: the birth of Kai energizes him by drawing something from deep inside him which he may not have known existed."[16]

In the poem "Regarding Wave" (35), Snyder brings together Buddhism, ecology, the living interpenetration of the entire world, and marriage. In the final lines he reaffirms his relationship with Masa, who continues to be an inspiration as wife, mother, and lover. At the bottom of the page are printed the three seed syllables of a Buddhist mantra. Julia Martin argues that here "the *Dharma* (the law, the way things are, the teachings of the Buddha) is articulated . . . in the pattern of this all-pervading energy." She finds Vāk's presence in the sound of the "shimmering bell" and suggests that the poem's ending with a mantra "is very appropriate, since Snyder's sources consider mantra to be the closest human articulation of Vāk; . . . the poem invites the audience to participate, not only in ideas *about* Vāk, the interconnectedness of phenomena, of 'self' and 'universe,' but also in the direct experience of union which reciting the mystic syllables is believed to evoke."[17]

"Long Hair"

The title of this section of *Regarding Wave* allies Snyder with the hippy movement of the 1960s and suggests that these poems will be more socially and politically oriented than those of the three "Regarding Wave" sections. Charles Molesworth notes that "Snyder speaks in *Earth House Hold* of long hair as a symbol of the acceptance of appetite and change, a willingness to go *through* the powers of nature."[18] Appropriately enough, the first poem is "Revolution in the Revolution in the Revolution" (39), the title a play on a Trotskyist slogan. Snyder begins with an axiom of the Maoist theory of guerrilla warfare in the first line and then extends it philosophically in the second. Here "back country" takes on the multiple resonances developed in Snyder's volume of that name, particularly its meaning of collective unconscious. In the second stanza, Snyder steps beyond all versions of Marxist theory by breaking with the anthropocentrism of revolutionary movements and positing that the environment has been far more exploited than any class of people. He then integrates in the third stanza the positions taken in the first two, and puts forward his ideal of "true Communionism" in opposition to both communism and capitalism. The poem ends by invoking the spiritual power of Buddhism.

In the title "It" (42–43), Snyder probably alludes to a book of the same name written by Alan Watts about the immanent spirituality that he found pervading the alternative culture/youth movement in the United States. In part, the point of Watts's book is to encourage people to stop worrying about defining and intellectualizing what was happening to them and society, go out and experience "it" for themselves, and go with the flow that "it" produces. Snyder indicates in a parenthetical statement that this poem came to him while reading Blake in a typhoon. William Blake, the most mystical and visionary of the British Romantic poets, also heavily emphasized experiencing spiritual states of being and wrote numerous poems concerned with the need to reintegrate the conscious and unconscious dimensions of the human psyche. Snyder begins by attempting to express the experience through language and comments at the end of the first stanza that "fields follow the laws of waves." In the next section of the poem, Snyder switches attention from the tropical storm to the book in hand and the movement of language between author and reader. Just as his immersion in the storm is participatory, so too is his immersion in the text, "mind-fronts"—like weather fronts that cause typhoons—"bite back at each other." Through this line Snyder links himself with the "puppy" mentioned in the first stanza. Both are responding to "storms," one the typhoon and the other Blake's poetry. The two experiences, physical and psychic, meld in the final stanza into a single energizing event, much in the same way that "myth" and "text" meld together at the end of Snyder's *Myths & Texts.* "It" remains undefined, experiential and all-encompassing, rather than intellectualized and limited.

"Meeting the Mountains" (60) may at first seem neither social nor political but merely a raw reportage of the infantile behavior of Snyder's son, Kai. It represents, however, another form of the kind of teaching by example practiced in *Earth House Hold.* Snyder captures the instinctive behavior of a baby, which when broken down into its separate components can be viewed as a type of ritual. The baby without consciousness greets the mountains and the waters in a ritualistic, reverential fashion. Perhaps most important about this behavior is that like some forms of baptism it requires immersion in the element itself.

In contrast, and more overtly political, "Before the Stuff Comes Down" (61) indicates Snyder's rather self-assured and dismissive attitude about the transiency of late capitalism in the United States as represented by a supermarket. While the previous poem contains a sense of permanence and itself has lasting interest thematically and aesthetically, the same cannot be said for "Before the Stuff Comes Down." Rather, it stands as a poem primarily of historical interest exemplary of the kind of revolution-around-the-corner optimism that suffused the 1960s counterculture. In the past twenty years, the "big E," a discount store, has survived with less difficulty than the "Turkey Buzzard" in overpopulated California. In some ways, the poem "Long Hair" (65–66) combines the best of "Meeting the Mountains" and "Before the Stuff

Comes Down.'' While it maintains the spirit of optimism of the second poem, humor replaces smugness and a commitment to long-term transformation replaces a mentality of instant revolution.

"Target Practice"

The brief poems of ''Target Practice'' have not received much critical attention, and if the volume ended with these it would be an unsatisfactory tapering off of the intensity of much of the rest of *Regarding Wave*. But Snyder saves a significant salvo for the last page, titled ''Civilization'' (84). Here he clearly sets forth his place and practice in the United States as an integrated opposition to the current aberration of human society called civilization. As he has remarked elsewhere, on the 40,000-year time line of human inhabitation of the planet, current social structures are a new and anomalous form of existence. In contrast to what he sees as a brief interlude of imbalance and disharmony in human evolution, Snyder affirms the inhabitory and archaic values that he outlined in *Earth House Hold* when he writes ''Fetch me my feathers and amber.'' In the second stanza of ''Civilization,'' suggesting that he is writing this poem while organizing ''Regarding Wave II'' or ''Eight Songs of Clouds and Water,'' he depicts himself as being pulled out of cultural/intellectual immersion into natural/experiential immersion through beholding a cricket. He concludes by delineating his ongoing individual practice as both poetic and physical, writing poems and heaping stones. His responsibilities to community, to family, and to place require both activities. In this poem, ''the interrelatedness of work and culture,'' according to Molesworth, ''is represented by the common image of a riverbed. . . . Poetry and the real work are both seen as ways of nourishing the community.''[19]

Molesworth's observation needs to be emended by noting that Snyder does not view these actions dualistically. Poetry is also a form of ''real work,'' but circumstances determine what kinds of work are more appropriate at a given moment. To pursue poetry when a flood is imminent would be acting irresponsibly in relation to family and community; to build a stone wall when a marriage ceremony needed a song would be equally irresponsible. "Civilization," like the rest of *Regarding Wave,* integrates these responsibilities and emphasizes especially seizing the opportunities to sing of achievements, events, and "miracles," such as birth, love, and marriage.

Notes

1. Katherine McNeill, *Gary Snyder, A Bibliography* (New York: Phoenix Bookshop, 1983) 43–45.

2. Gary Snyder, *Earth House Hold* (New York: New Directions, 1969) 80. Further page references to this volume are given in the text.

3. Uri Hertz, "An Interview with Gary Snyder," *Third Rail* 7 (1985–86) 52.

4. Sherman Paul, "From Lookout to Ashram: The Way of Gary Snyder," *Iowa Review* 1.3 and 1.4 (1970); edited version in Patrick D. Murphy, ed., *Critical Essays on Gary Snyder* (Boston: G. K. Hall, 1990) 64.

5. Gary Snyder, *The Real Work: Interviews & Talks, 1964–1979,* ed. Wm. Scott McLean (New York: New Directions, 1980) 137.

6. Gary Snyder, *Regarding Wave* (Iowa City: Windhover Press, 1969).

7. Gary Snyder, *Regarding Wave* (New York: New Directions, 1970). Further page references are to this edition and will be given in the text. Throughout this volume a glyph appears that looks like two three-pronged forks attached back-to-back. This is the three-pointed Thuderbolt of Vajrayana Buddhism. Its prongs stand for a series of tripartite relationships: unity of body, speech, mind; male, female, androgyne; husband, wife, child; and, moon, sun, fire; with the last three also tied to the three seed syllables of Om, Ah, and Hum.

8. Bob Steuding, *Gary Snyder* (Boston: Twayne, 1976) 135.

9. Bert Almon, "Buddhism and Energy in the Recent Poetry of Gary Snyder," *Mosaic* 11.1 (1970); rpt. in Murphy 82.

10. Steuding 149.

11. Snyder, *The Real Work* 89.

12. Katsunori Yamazato, "A Note on Japanese Allusions in Gary Snyder's Poetry," *Western American Literature* 18 (1983) 146–48.

13. David Robbins, "Gary Snyder's 'Burning Island,' " in *A Book of Rereadings in Recent American Poetry,* ed. Greg Kuzma (Lincoln, Neb.: Best Cellar Press, 1979); rpt. in Murphy 89–105. Further references to this work are given in the text.

14. Tom Lavazzi, "Pattern of Flux: The 'Torsion Form' in Gary Snyder's Poetry," *American Poetry Review* 18.4 (July/August 1989) 43.

15. Katsunori Yamazato, "Seeking a Fulcrum: Gary Snyder and Japan (1956–1975)," Ph.D. dissertation, University of California, Davis, 1987, 103.

16. Steuding 140.

17. Julia Martin, "True Communionism: Gary Snyder's Transvaluation of Some Christian Terminology," *Journal for the Study of Religion* (South Africa) 1.1 (1988) 69.

18. Charles Molesworth, *Gary Snyder's Vision: Poetry and the Real Work* (Columbia: University of Missouri Press, 1983) 87.

19. Molesworth 84–85.

CHAPTER SIX

Reinhabiting the Land:
Turtle Island, The Old Ways, and
Passage Through India

Turtle Island

By the beginning of the 1970s, Snyder had a solid body of poetry and prose in print and had clearly established his reputation among a sector of the American public. But as his decision not to distribute the chapbook *Manzanita* east of the Rockies suggests,[1] Snyder was mainly established on the West Coast. To the degree to which he was known elsewhere in the country, people tended to think of him as a California Beat poet. But his 1974 volume *Turtle Island* (which includes most of the poems in *Manzanita*) ended the regionalism of his reputation. From the beginning, it proved an extremely popular collection. Then, when it received the Pulitzer Prize for Poetry in 1975, Snyder was brought more fully to national attention. It remains today one of the best-selling contemporary collections of serious poetry in the United States.

More than his previous collections, *Turtle Island* clearly delineates Snyder as an inhabitant of the North American continent, someone here to stay and digging in to build the kind of earthhouse-hold he had recommended and about which he had theorized in his 1960s prose. The poems Snyder chose to collect here were written between 1969 and 1974, after his permanent return to the

United States, and they are arranged by section roughly according to when they were written. As Katsunori Yamazato sees it, " 'how to be' is the central question that Snyder asks and tries to answer throughout *Turtle Island*."[2] And Sherman Paul views inhabitation as Snyder's "climax of consciousness."[3]

Some critics have suggested that this volume should be understood as a post-Buddhist work, but that opinion overstates the case. The primary focus of *Turtle Island* is re-inhabitation, but Buddhism remains an integral aspect of Snyder's understanding and practice of a comprehensive philosophy of "how to be." In *Turtle Island,* the focus narrows in the sense that Snyder is primarily concerned with how to be *in North America,* which he conceptualizes in terms of an ancient Native American name: Turtle Island. As he says in the "Introductory Note": "the old/new name for the continent, based on many creation myths of the people who have been living here for millennia. . . . A name: that we may see ourselves more accurately on this continent. . . . The 'U.S.A.' and its states and counties are arbitrary and inaccurate impositions on what is really here."[4] In a sense, Snyder reaffirms his attitude toward the unreality of nation-states that he developed in his youth and affirms that Native American cultures remain a significant influence on his life. He renewed contact with Native Americans and resumed his study of their cultures as soon as he returned to California from Japan. In fact, by 1970 he had formulated his conception of North America as Turtle Island.[5]

Charles Molesworth, who approaches Snyder's work from a concern with his socio-political commitments and ideas, claims that "Snyder's vision largely ignores the social issues—that is, the mechanisms of daily life and such mundane concerns as urban experiences and bureaucratized work schemes—in favor of the political, such as the question of our relation to the environment, the blindness engendered by loyalty to the nation-state, and our allegiance to ideological systems based on domination and waste."[6] True, Snyder does not focus on "urbanization" and "work schemes," not because he ignores the mundane but because he includes a vision of an alternative, life-affirming mundane.

"Manzanita"

To develop an alternative vision of a balanced, sane daily life based on the history of this continent's *inhabitants* rather than its *immigrants,* Snyder initiates the "Manzanita" section of *Turtle Island* with "Anasazi" (3). This poem depicts the ecologically balanced life of the Native Americans who preceded the Hopi of the Southwest. Snyder follows this with "The Way West, Underground," outlining the dimensions of the circumpolar bear cult both in terms of its ancient origins and its alleged continuations in the present—"elder wilder goddesses reborn" (5). This poem, in turn, is followed by "Without." Here Snyder claims that "the path is whatever passes"; it is not an "end in itself" (6). "The Way West, Underground" and "Without" are followed by two poems relating specific practice in the present. In "The Dead by the Side of the Road" (7–8), Snyder emphasizes the tradition of using every part of an animal that has been killed and especially making use of roadkills—animals that have been hit by cars and trucks on the highway—as a modern adaptation of traditional practice. Such practice stands in direct contrast to the debased use and waste of animals practiced by modern agribusiness (which is criticized in "Steak" [10]) and sport hunting.

"I Went into the Maverick Bar" (9), the fifth poem, is one that has received considerable attention, both positive and negative. In it Snyder recognizes that his own heritage is the same as that of the people he encounters here (this topic is addressed again in "Dusty Braces" [75]). In the end, however, he emphasizes the difference between him and them: he denounces that cultural heritage because it has become destructive, xenophobic, and repressive. The speaker realizes that his responsibility to Turtle Island and to these people—although they are not yet ready to recognize or accept it—requires that he continue to promote his alternative vision. That this vision involves nothing short of complete social transformation is suggested by his defining the ''real work'' in terms of '' 'What is to be done,' '' the title of a major theoretical work by Lenin on the necessity of a Marxist revolution led by a vanguard party in Russia at the turn of the century.

If readers link these five poems rather than treating them separately, they can see them establishing a pattern in which ''Anasazi'' depicts a specific path in a particular place and time, a historical example of appropriate inhabitation. ''The Way West, Underground,'' then, links Native American experience, through the bear cult archetype, with other peoples and their related beliefs around the globe. These links provide the possibility for a new ''underground,'' a subversive movement, that may transform human relationship with the earth worldwide. This poem specifically embodies Snyder's call at the end of the ''Introductory Note'' to ''hark again to those roots, to see our ancient solidarity, and then to the work of being together on Turtle Island.'' The connection between the Anasazi people and the other cultures identified in ''The Way West'' is reinforced through the latter poem's last line, ''underground,'' echoing the image in the former poem of ''sinking deeper and deeper in earth'' (3), and the earth here is identified with the sacred.

While ''Anasazi'' depicts a specific historical practice and ''The Way West'' extends such practice globally, ''Without'' treats the issue of proper inhabitation in abstract terms heavily indebted to Buddhism and shamanism. The crucial Buddhist perception behind this poem is that of total interdependence and mutual co-creation of all entities in the world. In the universal process of co-creation an individual's vantage point is not a fixed, static position but a momentary node in the ongoing transformation of energy. As a result, determining the proper forms of right practice requires attention to localized specifics—''the path is whatever passes''—because diversity is a crucial feature of healthy ecosystems worldwide.

Any practice, then, to be right must be attuned to the features of the local processes in which it will take place. One such proper path or right practice is depicted by Snyder in ''The Dead by the Side of the Road.'' This practice, though, seems somewhat out of time and not necessarily specific to its location because of the generality of the actions depicted. ''I Went into the Maverick Bar'' brings all of this explicitly home. It takes the speaker into the immediacy of the present, the problems and the promise of responsible behavior here on Turtle Island.

In ''The Bath'' (12–14), Snyder returns to one of the themes dominating *Regarding Wave* and evident earlier as one of his concerns in the Japan poems in *Riprap:* harmonious family life. If family is the practice hall, as he has remarked, then his vision of a new, more harmonious, ecologically balanced culture for North America must include a functional family. ''The Bath'' accomplishes that inclusion. As Julia Martin notes, ''to give this attention to bathing indicates a deliberate making of community, and a definition of family-as-energy-network that is radically different from the familiar nuclear structure. The model of interrelationships which this offers extends in other poems to 'The Great Family,' to include those who are not necessarily blood-relations, and may even be non-human''[7] (Martin is referring here to ''Prayer for the Great Family'' [24–25]). The interrelationship consists of both social and ecological harmony, in process through time since the family will change as the children grow and as each person's body ages. Here and in ''Prayer for the Great Family'' there should also be noted the religious, sacramental quality of the activity and the tone of each poem. Snyder makes this explicit through the refrain about ''our body,'' which echoes the language of the Catholic communion service but renders it plural: each body is our body through mutual co-creation and interdependence.

''Spel Against Demons,'' reprinted from *The Fudo Trilogy* chapbook (1973), displays a different dimension of Snyder's religious concerns in *Turtle Island*. Very different from the verse that has preceded it in the volume, "Spel Against Demons" is, as Ya-mazato explains it, "a poem that attempts to exorcise the demonic forces inside the civilization by introducing a powerful figure from Buddhism, 'ACHALA the Immovable' (*Fudōmyō-ō,* in Japanese)." Interestingly enough, Snyder derived his knowledge of this *Shingon* Buddhist deity by way of *Shugendo,* which "originally was a nature-worship religion that borrowed its theoretical basis from *Shingon.*"[8] At the end of the poem is a Buddhist mantra attributed to Fudōmyō-ō, which is translated in the "Smokey the Bear Sutra" by Snyder as meaning "I dedicate myself to the universal diamond be this raging fury destroyed."[9] Snyder here both seriously and playfully adapts and updates the Buddhist mantra to emphasize the interrelationship of the spiritual and social dimensions of his vision for a new way of life.

That the spiritual is not adequate unto itself Snyder makes explicit through the next two poems in *Turtle Island.* In "Front Lines" (18), the forest is depicted as a victim threatened by contemporary America. The "chainsaw growls" like a stalking predator. Due to wet weather, logging stops and "The trees breathe." This description is literally true in that trees do breathe, but one should also read this figuratively, as if they are able to relax. But such relaxation is a mistake. The third stanza displays an angry reaction by the speaker to jets overhead because they represent the entire economic empire with its military might that threatens the trees and the land. To emphasize this point, Snyder spells out the enemy as "Amerika," a popular epithet during the 1960s used to identify the U.S. with fascism. He combines this name with an organic metaphor that likens the U.S. economy to an obese man with cholesterol-clogged arteries. The fifth stanza then combines with the end of the third to sandwich this image of decadence between two depictions of the "rape" of Mother Earth.

In "Front Lines" the individual working the bulldozer is not treated as the "enemy." Here, rather, his wrath is reserved for the man from the city, who is engineering this destruction without having any direct contact with the environment that he is having razed for financial gain. The poem ends by locating the forest in both space and time, through its identification with the vast reaches of Turtle Island and those inhabitants who have been there for thousands of years. Snyder demands of himself and the reader that they take a stand, here and now, against further devastation of the natural world. For Snyder, defense of the forests is both a planetary issue, in relation to the decimation of the rain forests and their potential impact on the greenhouse effect, and a local one. His area of California borders the Tahoe National Forest, and that part of the country has been badly damaged in the past by both hydraulic gold mining and clear cutting of forests. The poem, then, reflects not only a general political stance but also a specific one speaking to the local defense of nature in which he and his neighbors have been engaged. Snyder remarked in a mid-1970s interview that "it's the eternal moment. I think in those terms, but I also think in terms of organic evolution, and from that standpoint we have a critical time now in which decisions are being made which will have long reaching effects on the survival of many forms of life."[10]

"Control Burn" (19) continues the issue of forestry practices, but here the literal is secondary to the figurative. Snyder depicts actual Indian behavior in California; he does so, not so much to teach readers about the native activity of controlled burns but in order to use it as an image for the kind of purgation that American culture requires. In effect, he argues that American society has become cluttered with too much "logging slash" and secondary growth that renders the entire ecosystem vulnerable to catastrophe. "A hot clean / burn," a sudden upheaval or revolutionary social transformation, would clear away all of this tangled undergrowth that obscures vision and threatens the "tall and clear" stands of trees normal to a climax forest, i.e., a forest in mature ecological balance.

"The Call of the Wild" (21–23) addresses the issue of human beings threatening nature, as did "Front Lines." But here the tone is more sorrowful than wrathful as Snyder expresses concern more for what the next generation will lose than for what his own may suffer. Each section consists of a mini-narrative. The first focuses on the life of an old man who has been a "native" but clearly has never become an inhabitant, has never established a relationship with the world around him. He refuses to hear the coyotes "singing"; to him they only "howl," and so he will have them killed by the "Government / Trapper." The old man will never realize his loss, but Snyder's children will: "My sons will lose this / Music they have just started / To love." Snyder also indicates that establishing a harmonious relationship with one's environment is not automatic. The sons are only just starting to learn, but it is not simply a matter of time or else the old man would also share that love. It is, instead, a matter of attitude, attention, and interdependence.

The second section tells the story of city hippies who move to the countryside as a result of a psychedelic religious impulse rather than out of a commitment to nature and inhabitation.[11] They commit acts as destructive as the old man's: choosing inappropriate housing, trying to transplant a life-style from another bioregion, and selling their trees out of ignorance. They too fear the coyote, because, as Snyder implies, they fear the unconscious, "the wild," inside themselves. The choice of hippies, younger than Snyder himself, indicates that clearly the problem cannot be assigned to a single generation. In the third section Snyder expands his mournful critique from individuals to government. In what is virtually a parable, he develops an analogy between the Vietnam war—the U.S. attempts at jungle defoliation and eradication of peasant villages and life-styles—and the modern scientific/technological attack on the earth through pesticides, chemical fertilizers, synthetics, and sterile, artificial housing. This "war against earth" will not only destroy the ecology but will also result in "no place // A Coyote could hide.'' Snyder's capitalization clarifies that he is not speaking here of one animal but that he is using Coyote symbolically to represent the spirit within, the unconscious that connects humans with all other sentient beings.

The ''envoy'' of the poem stresses in an elegiac tone that nothing guarantees the survival of the human-animal spirit. By implication, those who would seek to preserve that spirit must act to defend Coyote and his habitat. L. Edwin Folsom's observation about the volume as a whole seems relevant here: ''Snyder announces the opening of the frontier again and attempts to push it eastward, to reverse America's historical process, to urge the wilderness to grow back into civilization to release the stored energy from layers below us.''[12]

Clearly, the middle poems of the ''Manzanita'' section of *Turtle Island* take on a tone that, if not apocalyptic, certainly registers a sense of impending crisis. But the section does not end on that note. Snyder circles back to the more long-range kind of perception suggested in the first several poems as he approaches the section's close. ''Prayer for the Great Family'' emphasizes human, ecological, and cosmic interdependent harmony and harkens back again to the old ways of Turtle Island's original inhabitants. ''Source'' (26) begins to suggest that the activist who left the ''Maverick Bar'' to resume his real work should learn to imitate the manzanita, a second-growth bush that proliferates rapidly in mined-off and clear-cut land. ''Source'' indicates that manzanita is hospitable to other plants and creatures, working with, not against, its bioregional co-inhabitants. At the end, Snyder also suggests that the plant proliferates because it has learned to grow not only with sunlight but also with ''that black light'' of the night stars. If one associates this image with the political notion of the ''underground'' implied in ''The Way West,'' Snyder can be seen to be recommending that the proponents of the new culture work in darkness, in quiet, in out-of-the-way places, as they build strength, extend their communities, widen their nets, and deepen their roots.

In the poem that provides the title for the "Manzanita" section, Snyder suggests that the manzanita plant itself can serve as part of the healing magic necessary for reinhabitation. This magic will allow him and others to realize the true size of the many little signs by which the Earth can be seen to be regenerating itself. Looking at "Manzanita" along with "Charms" (27 and 28), Charles Molesworth argues that these two poems "show how the reinhabitation of the land will be aided by songs of knowledge and community."[13] These are precisely the kinds of poems that Snyder has arranged into the second part of *Turtle Island*, "Magpie's Song." This section contains thirty-one poems displaying a much greater diversity of styles, tones, lengths, and content than to be found in "Manzanita."

"Magpie's Song"

"Night Herons" (35–36) addresses in some detail ideas present in the several poems that precede it. Snyder, on a walk with friends down by the wharf area, meditates on the presence of the "night herons" in San Francisco. As he notes the machinery of modern life—some in use and some abandoned, like "the rusty island prison" on Alcatraz—he also gradually realizes the continuous presence of animals who are managing to inhabit this area, just as the people do. As he wonders about the herons' return, he suddenly realizes that their return is no more or no less peculiar than his own and that he enjoys being here amidst the machinery of the city. Part of the "joy" he feels, which he assumes the other animals feel, comes from the experience of survival: growing older, toughening up, and gradually being eaten away. Here, then, Snyder feels a sense of self-renewal of humans and other animals in a mutually sustaining community.

"The Uses of Light" (39) shifts from the meditative mode into a playful, rhyming kind of poetry. Yamazato believes that in this poem Snyder extends compassion for other beings to include the inanimate as well as the animate. The poem's indebtedness to Buddhism is evident because ''the principal Buddha in the Avatamsaka sutra is Vairocana (the Sun Buddha), who is depicted in that sutra as the center of the universe''; and, further, '' 'stones,' 'trees,' 'moth,' 'deer,' and people in this world are all interrelated and constitute a harmonious whole while *illumined* by the spiritual light that emanates from the Sun Buddha.''[14]

But it is not necessary to conceptualize the poem in these terms to determine the importance of ''light.'' The last point made in ''Facts'' is that ''our primary source of food is the sun'' (31). In terms of the function of photosynthesis in the food chain, the human as well as many other animals' need for sunlight to exist, and the necessity of solar radiation for the composition of Earth's atmosphere, it could be said from the viewpoint of basic ecological science that everything on the planet is interrelated. But the point of the first four stanzas of ''The Uses of Light'' is not simply to get readers to appreciate the role of sunlight in their daily lives; if so the fifth stanza would be superfluous. That final stanza is based on an old Chinese saying about expanding one's perceptual horizons and suggests that a slight readjustment can lead to a significantly expanded awareness. From the perspective of the final stanza, then, the rhymes about light serve primarily to get readers to reconceptualize the mundane in terms of its complex interconnections. And Snyder encourages such re-perception in part by having each stanza presented from the point of view of a different component of the natural world: rock, vegetation, insect, and mammal.

Snyder expands on this issue of re-perception in ''By Frazier Creek Falls'' (41). Here, however, the point of view remains human to human. Snyder attempts to immerse readers in the image of nature he portrays so that they will not learn from the poem so much as they will imitate it by gaining direct experience. For the second half of the poem to mean anything to readers, they would have had to have experienced the equivalent of the first half of the poem. In this second half Snyder lectures against the kind of transcendence of the physical found in so many American religions as well as in its romantic and idealist philosophies. "We *are* it" insists on not just recognizing interrelatedness but on making that the central fact of existence. If one comes to comprehend that point then "clothes," "tools," and the rest of the trappings of civilization are viewed in terms of "the path is whatever passes" ("Without" 6). They are accessories, not essentials.

A person who has assimilated the messages of such poems as "Without," "The Uses of Light," and "By Frazier Creek Falls" should have no problem espousing the attitude found in "It Pleases" (44). As the dateline indicates, Snyder wrote this poem on a visit to Washington, D.C., in November 1973. As in "Night Herons," Snyder finds the soaring bird overhead in D.C. the most solidly real aspect of the scene before him. Emblematic of wild nature, it soars over what human society has imagined to be the center of world power. But Snyder declares that "The center of power is nothing!" because "The World does what it pleases." Wild nature goes on about its own business, indifferent to the halls of civil power. But the exclamation also contains an ironic joke in that Buddhism considers emptiness, the Void, to be at the center of all things. So that to call something the "center" is to define it as emptiness. Washington, D.C., in effect, is merely a form into which people infuse power through their allegiances and affiliations.

For many critics, "Mother Earth: Her Whales" (47–49) is Snyder's most grandly accomplished poem in this section. As Hwa Yol Jung and Petee Jung have noted, Snyder wrote this poem about a month after he attended the United Nations conference on the human environment in Stockholm and published it in the *New York Times* (July 13, 1972): "It began with a terse foreword in which he said that everyone came to Stockholm not to give but rather to take, not to save the planet but to argue about how to divide it up. . . . The poem meant to defend all the creatures of the earth.''[15] The last sentence fairly well sums up the poem's theme, but its structure and style are also worth analyzing.

The opening stanza of ''Mother Earth: Her Whales'' describes activity without a designated narrator and ends with the participle ''watching,'' which while specific to the sparrow may apply to the owl and lizard as well, all of which appear in these four lines. Any or all of them, then, may be the speaker of the next stanza, which consists of a reverential chant that could serve as a grace before meals. The third stanza provides a sharp contrast to this reverential, nurturing prayer of interpenetrating existence and is clearly presented from the viewpoint of a human narrator. The ''Brazil'' that is named does not identify a bioregional or ecological entity but stands only for the imposition of arbitrary human boundaries on the Amazon watershed. The government spokesman displays a nature-as-resource mentality that goes hand in hand with such boundaries and which the narrator obviously abhors. These first three stanzas focus on the land and its inhabitants.

The fourth and fifth stanzas turn to the oceans and the island nation of Japan. The fourth, paralleling the first two stanzas of the poem, describes the behavior of whales with respect and awe. In contrast, the fifth stanza condemns Japan, as the third did Brazil, for its slaughter of whales and its pollution of the sea. The sixth and seventh stanzas replicate this pattern, this time attending to the river watersheds of eastern Asia. Snyder here adds a historical dimension to indicate that species extermination and agricultural degradation of bioregions are not simply twentieth-century phenomena. It is also worth noting that he attacks in the seventh stanza the basic concept of anthropocentrism that guides the philosophies of virtually all of modern culture. The eighth stanza includes the United States and Canada in its circle of condemnation.

At the ninth stanza, the negative critique is suddenly interrupted by a declaration of solidarity. ''The People,'' consonant with Native American beliefs, means here all animals living together, not just humans. With that cry for solidarity, Snyder returns in the next stanza to his attack on all of the "civilized" governments represented in Stockholm, all of whom failed to "speak for the green of the leaf" (48).[16] Snyder then conflates the image of governmental resource managers as "vultures" with an old English ballad in which the birds pluck out the eyes of a "slain knight" (47). This overlay of imagery implies that no honor and no respect for others exist among the representatives of civilization. The ballad describes not animal but human behavior as rapacious and devouring. Snyder concludes on a note of hope by returning to the owl, the lizard, the whales, i.e., the community of other peoples, who are the "wild" with which he will identify himself. They are the ones who know "how to be" in the "living light." When the poet beholds civilization he is repulsed and disgusted; fortunately, if "It Pleases" is accurate, civilization is not the main thing going on anyway.

"Straight-Creek—Great Burn" (52–53) continues this positive identification with the wild even as it harkens back to earlier poems, such as "Control Burn." Sherman Paul finds this a particularly compelling poem not only for what it does in its own right but also for the ways in which it demonstrates Snyder's maturity and growth. Paul thinks of it not so much in relation to the rest of *Turtle Island* as in relation to the numerous other poems that Snyder has written about the advent of spring. As he sees it, Snyder is "more meditative now, and not solitary. . . . his attention—*watching* is now the primary activity of participation (one of the ways he is teaching his sons)—is both remarkably close and wide, aware."[17] As many of the poems that have preceded it in *Turtle Island* suggest, "watching" becomes an extremely significant form of action, if the person so engaged opens him or herself up to changed perception. Without careful observation one simply cannot become an inhabitant.

There is also a significant political theme developed in this poem, which does not come clear until almost the end:

never a leader,
all of one swift

empty
dancing mind. (53)

Nature contains a high degree of complex organization and interaction, as demonstrated by the interaction of rock and water,
mountains and rivers, depicted in the first five stanzas. In subsequent lines, people are introduced "resting" and "watching" this
complexity. That introduction is followed by the last four stanzas
on the intricate, interactive dancing flight of a flock of birds. They
too are highly organized and complex, but their leadership consists
of "mind" rather than governmental structures, civilizations, psychological strictures, or other trapping of the modern nation-state.
That readers should establish such an identification between the
people and the birds in the poem is suggested by the parallel of the
last two lines: "they settle down. / end of poem" (53). Both the
action of the birds and that of the poet culminate simultaneously.

"Bedrock" (64) is much simpler than some of the poems from
"Magpie's Song"; nevertheless, it is an important part of this section. Snyder has so far been emphasizing that true learning comes
from the rest of nature, particularly wild nature. But here he turns
back to other humans for education, specifically his wife, to whom
the poem is dedicated. The first stanza emphasizes their general
satisfaction and their breaking free from intellectualizing and ratio-
nalizing thought. In this context, Snyder asks: "teach me to be
tender" (64). If the poem ended with their having tea, we might
consider it simply sentimental, but it does not. It ends by admitting
that they "laugh" *and* "grieve." In the midst, then, of his denun-
ciations of the failures of civilization and his wisdom-figure teaching of his readers to learn from wild nature, he pauses to admit his
own weaknesses and to suggest that everyone must continue learning in general, especially learning to love each other better. The

title of the poem, then, can be read as a double pun: one, "bedrock" meaning foundation, with love playing that role here; two, bedrock as rocky bed, meaning the difficulties of marriage. "The Dazzle" (65), by the way, functions as something of a postscript to "Bedrock," celebrating the mysteries of birth that result from the heterosexual love idealized in that poem. The two also echo *Regarding Wave*.

The poem "Magpie's Song" (69) would make little sense if it appeared any earlier in *Turtle Island*. By this point, though, it resonates strongly with the poems that precede it and in a sense summarizes this second section of the volume. The initial stanza sets the scene: the speaker in the desert at sunup, sitting by railroad tracks and listening to the coyotes singing. The earlier poems have rendered them a heavily laden symbol. Magpie then sings a song, which begins by identifying human and bird as brothers and invoking a magical stone, turquoise, the symbolism of which Snyder has already developed in "The Blue Sky." The breeze that Magpie calls on the human to smell may be said to represent the "wave" function of wisdom as it is passed on from being to being—the last line of "Ethnobotany" is instructive in this regard: "Taste all, and hand the knowledge down" (51). But most important is the assurance provided by this representative of wild nature that the speaker need not fear "What's ahead" (69). Snyder suggests at poem's end that as long as one keeps the wisdom of wild nature firmly in mind, there is no need to fear the future.

As Michael Castro sees it, "the capitalized 'Mind' in the next to the last line suggests the 'original' or 'biomass' mind. The poem itself should be seen as a modern attempt at a 'shaman song' that tries to put us into contact with that 'Mind.' It brings back from the mystical experience the voice of the nonhuman or extrahuman and shares it with the community."[18] "Magpie's Song" reinforces the overall positive and confident tone of this section, and through the inclusion of Coyote, counters the pessimistic tone sounded in "The Call of the Wild." At the same time, it demonstrates Snyder's increasingly self-conscious assumption of the role of a white shaman for modern Turtle Island.

"For the Children"

In "For the Children," the third section of *Turtle Island,* Snyder assumes the function of a shaman to a greater degree than in the earlier parts, here passing on wisdom and reassurance. This section begins with "O Waters" (73), which is another of the many ritualized prayer-poems of the volume. It calls on the waters to "wash us, me" as the speaker observes the way in which the mountains and the waters of the world are moving and flowing, following the wave function of the interdependent energy-transfer-network. The poem ends by defining this network as a "sangha" (Buddhist fellowship) of the entire planet.

"Tomorrow's Song" (77), after announcing that "The USA slowly lost its mandate" because it failed to include the nonhuman in its definition of democracy, attempts to prepare the poem's readers for the future. Snyder predicates this future upon the continent's return to its status as Turtle Island through people adopting some kind of inhabitory culture based largely on the old ways. Snyder implies that the future will be built on the basis of a post-industrial, post-fossil-fuel economy that adapts many of the labor and cultural practices of the continent's original inhabitants. People will be capable of building this future Turtle Island because they will have established a set of nature-based values serving "wilderness" and the Earth as mother.

But to be able to participate in preparing for such a rebuilding, the future citizens of Turtle Island will need to know the history of this land they seek to re-inhabit. To that end, Snyder provides the poem "What Happened Here Before" (78–81), which recapitulates the history of the western slope of Turtle Island starting three hundred million years ago. The first stanza, then, concerns the continent's earliest geological history. The second stanza, eighty million years ago, continues with attention to the formation of the

Western mountains and sedimentation of gold there. The third stanza, three million years ago, tells of the formation of the waters that make up some of the major rivers, the Feather, the Bear, and the Yuba, of the northern California watershed around the Nevada City area.

Then, at the forty-thousand-year mark, Snyder claims people began to appear, the first human inhabitants of a land already heavily populated by other animals. According to Snyder, "the white man" really only arrived in the area with the Gold Rush, one hundred and twenty-five years ago—a last-second smudge on the region's time line. In contrast to the stanza on the first natives, this stanza makes it very clear that the "white man" did not come to inhabit, to adapt himself to the land and the creatures already there, human and nonhuman, but to make all else adapt to him. And therein began the trouble. In response Snyder declares: "the land belongs to itself" (80).

Only in the final stanzas does Snyder indicate what generated this complex explanation of the history of the land he inhabits. He and his sons have apparently been out camping and they ask, no doubt quite innocently, "who are we?" The poem emphatically declares that that question cannot be answered without also answering "where are we?" And for Snyder, the state of being an inhabitant is what determines the state of one's being, as he declares in emphatic capitals: "WE SHALL SEE WHO KNOWS HOW TO BE." The final line, "Bluejay screeches from a pine," suggests that the bird rather than, or as well as, the human is the one announcing that challenge in response to the "military jets" overhead. As Castro understands it, the poem is written from the continent's point of view, and this would accord with the ambiguity as to whether the bluejay or the poet is the speaker of that militant challenge. Further, Castro claims that "Turtle Island is thus presented to us as a vital thing, vaster and longer-lived than many or any of its species. When we achieve an understanding and an appreciation of the depth and scope of its life, the poem's implicit message states, we can begin to come into proper relationship to our land."[19]

"Toward Climax" (82–85), which follows up on "What Happened Here Before," begins to answer the question of "who knows how to be." It does so by contrasting the way of life of the culture that has produced the military jets that Snyder and his sons hear overhead with the way of life of the inhabitory peoples, human and nonhuman, of the "old/new" Turtle Island. The contrast is presented most starkly in part four, in which the practice of mass slaughter, mainly by aerial bombardment, is juxtaposed to a primitive perception of "virgin / Forest." It will be remembered that maintaining a climax forest versus clear-cutting is the dividing line that Snyder announces in "Front Lines." As with the other sections of this volume, Snyder shifts into an optimistic and virtually utopian mood at the end of "For the Children," with the poem by that title and "As for Poets."

"Plain Talk"

Despite the diversity of styles and tones displayed in *Turtle Island,* what stays in the mind of many readers is a note of urgency, a confrontational directness, and a political activism never so overt or didactic in Snyder's previous writing. This immediacy is reflected particularly in the fourth part of the volume. The most significant of these five prose pieces is the first one, "Four Changes." This essay had already been read widely prior to its publication here. The original version was distributed in photocopy form in early 1969. Later that year, *Earth Read Out,* a Berkeley environmental newsletter, printed a revised version. Then again that same year, Robert Shapiro in association with Alan Watts printed fifty thousand copies of the essay in broadside form and distributed it without charge nationwide. Eventually, another eleven thousand copies were printed.[20] Nearly sixty thousand copies of this essay, then, were in circulation prior to its book publication. What Snyder has reprinted in *Turtle Island* consists of the 1969 revised version with more recent comments interpolated.

Snyder presents in this essay a clear, concise overview of his social philosophy. The other essays continue in this same vein. The very brief " 'Energy Is Eternal Delight' " (the title comes from the Romantic poet William Blake) deals with the energy crisis and Native American resistance to uranium mining in the Southwest. "The Wilderness" continues with a focus on Native American ways, serving as a sort of prelude to the essays in *The Old Ways.* Snyder's main concern here is with getting "what the Sioux Indians called the creeping people, and the standing people, and the flying people, and the swimming people—into the councils of government" (108).

The last two essays are more explicitly linked to the poetry of the volume. "What's Meant By 'Here' " provides a prose explanation of the present condition of the land depicted in "What Happened Here Before." And the final essay, "On 'As for Poets,' " explains the function of poetry in relation to Snyder's own beliefs and commitments, taking the reader back to "Four Changes." In the introduction to that first essay, Snyder makes a remark that emphasizes once again the relationship between immediate action and ongoing practice: "My Teacher once said to me, —become one with the knot itself, til it dissolves away. —sweep the garden.—any size" (91). He confirms that Zen practice continues to guide his way in the world. Later in the essay he defines the garden and the sweeping: "no transformation without our feet on the ground. Stewardship means, for most of us, find your place on the planet, dig in, and take responsibility from there. . . . Get a sense of workable territory, learn about it, and start acting point by point" (101). And one form of such acting is writing poems, which Snyder links with the issues of energy and community at the end of "On 'As for Poets' ": "Poetry is for all men and women. The power within—the more you give, the more you have to give—will still be our source when coal and oil are long gone, and atoms are left to spin in peace" (114).

While critics such as Charles Altieri have expressed dissatisfaction with *Turtle Island* as a weakening of Snyder's aesthetic strengths because of its privileging of politics and prophecy,[21] Charles Molesworth claims that "taken together, and with the remarkable prose essays as well, the three sections of poetry in *Turtle Island* form a whole that advances Snyder's work well beyond the objectivist poetics of the early books and the political suppositions of *Earth House Hold*."[22] Sherman Paul seems to respond to some of the complaints about *Turtle Island* being more political than poetic when he concludes that "political action, in fact, may be the most significant measure of [Snyder's] love because learning to love has taught him what to defend. It has also made him joyous. This political book is remarkably joyous, and serene; hence, its authenticity."[23] Finally, Hwa Yol Jung and Petee Jung conclude their study of Snyder's ecopiety with a remark that seems eminently suited to summing up *Turtle Island:* "The political mandate of Snyder's ecopoetry is Communionism. . . . Communionism is first and foremost the way of seeking a deep sense of communion with myriads of natural things on earth, who are also called 'peoples,' without any facile dualism and unnecessary hierarchism of any kind."[24]

The Old Ways *and* Passage Through India

In the years between the success of *Turtle Island* and the appearance of another full-length book of poetry, Snyder published two volumes of prose, and a collection of previously published interviews, *Gary Snyder: The Real Work: Interviews & Talks 1964–1979*, edited by Wm. Scott McLean, was released by New Directions in 1980. *The Old Ways: Six Essays* was published by City Lights Books in 1977.[25] It has remained continuously in print since then but is generally treated in the same way that *Earth*

House Hold often is, primarily as a reference work for interpreting Snyder's poetry. Of the six essays, the four most substantive ones are based on talks given from 1974 through 1976. In many respects, the volume can be read as continuing the task undertaken by the "Plain Talk" section of *Turtle Island*: to clarify Snyder's beliefs and commitments.

A somewhat different version of *Passage Through India,* published in 1983, originally appeared as "Now India" in the Spring 1972 issue of the little magazine *Caterpillar.* Despite the fact that the 1983 publication by Grey Fox Press afforded this work wider circulation, it seems to have remained of little critical interest. It records Snyder's impressions during the six-month visit he and Joanne Kyger made to India from December 1961 through April 1962. Snyder concludes his 1983 foreword with these words: "The sharp-tongued, sharp-eyed village men and women, skinny with hard work and never a big fat meal to eat a whole lifetime, live under an eternal sky of stars, and on a beginningless earth. They might need aid-dollars or aid-food, but they don't need or want pity or disgust. An anvil the spirit is pounded finer on, India. Skinny, and flashing eyes."[26] These journal entries provide background particularly on the "Kālī" section of *The Back Country.* But for those concerned with re-inhabitation and the message of *Turtle Island, The Old Ways* proves a far more valuable book.

The two short pieces in the middle of *The Old Ways* are primarily meaningful to people familiar with the North Beach scene in San Francisco that they address. The first essay, "The Yogin and the Philosopher," was originally presented at a 1974 conference "The Rights of the Non-Human." Of particular interest here is Snyder's delineation of what has been termed the Great Subculture and is hinted at in the *Turtle Island* poem, "The Way West, Underground." Snyder relates the Eastern concept of the Yogin with the Native American and primitive culture concept of the shaman, once more seeking a syncretic blend translatable into one of the roles of the modern poet. Snyder concludes that "one of the few

modes of speech that gives us access to that other yogic or shamanistic view (in which all is one and all is many, and the many
are all precious) is poetry or song'' (13–14). As Snyder has said
elsewhere, he views here the roles of the yogin, the shaman, and
the poet as being identical when it comes to the task of speaking
for the nonhuman to humans.

''The Politics of Ethnopoetics,'' originally a talk given at an ethnopoetics conference in Milwaukee in 1975, addresses an issue
very much under debate in anthropological and poetic circles
throughout the 1970s and into the 1980s. Snyder opens this essay
by taking a clear-cut position on what politics means to him: ''This
'politics' is fundamentally the question of what occidental and industrial technological civilization is doing to the earth'' (15). In
explaining his understanding of ethnopoetics, Snyder goes to some
length to define the people whose poetics would be studied as
those who practice ecosystem cultures rather than biosphere culture, the latter being defined as the culture of centralized states
that can wreck one ecosystem and ''keep moving on'' to exploit
others (21). What has probably attracted most attention in this essay, however, is not Snyder's definition of ethnopoetics but his pro-
motion of the Gaia hypothesis popularized by James Lovelock,
Sidney Epton, Lyn Margulis, and others. In brief, it ''is a bio-
chemists' hypothesis, that the whole of the biosphere is one living
organism which has strategically programmed its evolution for 3
billion years, including producing us'' (39). Snyder concludes that
the study of ethnopoetics only makes sense if it assists contemporary peoples in re-inhabiting the planet along the lines of the old
ways, that is, along the lines of working ''toward climax.''

The fifth essay, ''Re-Inhabitation,'' is another major piece in
line with the first two of the volume. In many aspects it recapitulates points made in the first essay, with special emphasis on defining the term ''inhabitation'' and pointing toward the kinds of
practices that need to be implemented, with a bit of autobiography
thrown in along the way. In the last essay, ''The Incredible Sur-

vival of Coyote,'' Snyder emphasizes once again his indebtednessess to Native American cultures for his own beliefs and practices. This essay also helps to explain the strong presence of Coyote throughout so much of his poetry, from *Myths & Texts* through *Turtle Island*. Snyder explains near the end of his talk that ''Coyote, as I said, was interesting to me and some of my colleagues because he spoke to us of place, because he clearly belonged to the place and became almost like a guardian, a protector spirit. The other part of it has to come out of something inside us. The fascination with the trickster'' (83–84).

While Snyder clearly developed his understanding and use of Native American practices in his poetry and prose in the 1970s, he also maintained his commitment to Buddhist values. His growing commitment to place, as suggested by the preceding quotation, would not, however, be fully realized in his poetry until the 1980s.

Notes

1. Katherine McNeill, *Gary Snyder, A Bibliography* (New York: Phoenix Bookshop, 1983) 68–69.

2. Katsunori Yamazato, ''How to Be in This Crisis: Gary Snyder's Cross-Cultural Vision in *Turtle Island*,'' in *Critical Essays on Gary Snyder*, ed. Patrick D. Murphy (Boston: G. K. Hall, 1990) 230.

3. Sherman Paul, *In Search of the Primitive: Rereading David Antin, Jerome Rothenberg, and Gary Snyder* (Baton Rouge: Louisiana State University Press, 1986) 274.

4. Gary Snyder, *Turtle Island* (New York: New Directions, 1974). All references are to this edition and are given in the text.

5. Katsunori Yamazato, ''Seeking a Fulcrum: Gary Snyder and Japan (1956–1975),'' Ph.D. dissertation, University of California, Davis, 1987, 118–19.

6. Charles Molesworth, *Gary Snyder's Vision: Poetry and the Real Work* (Columbia: University of Missouri Press, 1983) 8.

7. Julia Martin, ''True Communionism: Gary Snyder's Transvaluation of Some Christian Terminology,'' *Journal for the Study of Religion* (South Africa) 1.1 (1988): 66.

8. Yamazato, ''How to Be'' 236.

9. Gary Snyder, *The Fudo Trilogy* (Berkeley: Shaman Drum, 1973) n.p. Fudōmyō-ō appears in all three of the poems printed here; hence the title of the chapbook.

Reinhabiting the Land

10. Ekbert Faas, "Gary Snyder," *Towards a New American Poetics: Essays & Interviews* (Santa Barbara: Black Sparrow Press, 1979) 109–10.

11. Snyder comments on the kind of people depicted here in Faas 113.

12. L. Edwin Folsom, "Gary Snyder's Descent to Turtle Island: Searching for Fossil Love," *Western American Literature* 15 (1980) 109.

13. Molesworth 101. While I agree with his general point, I disagree with Molesworth's appreciation of "Charms," which I think is marred by a sexist attitude.

14. Yamazato, "How to Be" 239.

15. Hwa Yol Jung and Petee Jung, "Gary Snyder's Ecopiety," *Environmental History Review* 14.3 (1990) 76.

16. The Jungs note that Snyder considered the Hopi delegation the only exception to this behavior.

17. Paul 276.

18. Michael Castro, "Gary Snyder: The Lessons of *Turtle Island*," from *Interpreting the Indian: Twentieth-Century Poets and the American Indian* (Albuquerque: University of New Mexico Press, 1984); rpt. in Murphy 139.

19. Castro 134–35.

20. This publication history is documented in McNeill 47–50.

21. Charles Altieri, "Gary Snyder's *Turtle Island:* The Problem of Reconciling the Roles of Seer and Prophet," *boundary 2* 4 (1976): 761–77.

22. Molesworth 104.

23. Paul 282.

24. Jung and Jung 84.

25. Gary Snyder, *The Old Ways: Six Essays* (San Francisco: City Lights Books, 1977). All page references to this edition are given in the text.

26. Gary Snyder, *Passage Through India* (San Francisco: Grey Fox Press, 1983) x-xi.

CHAPTER SEVEN

Handing Down the Practice: *Axe Handles* and *Left Out in the Rain*

Axe Handles

Often after poets have received a major award, such as the Pulitzer Prize, they quickly bring out another volume of poetry. Snyder did not follow this trend. Nearly ten years passed after the appearance of *Turtle Island* before Snyder published another full-length collection of poems. In 1983, he produced *Axe Handles,* with a new publisher, North Point Press of San Francisco, and with a new tone. While Charles Molesworth in a review is right when he claims that "the central tension here is the same that animated *Turtle Island* (1974): how can we carry on the meaningful transmission of community and culture against the threatening background of ecological perversity and vast geological and cosmic processes," it does not seem entirely accurate to speak of "tension" so much as of continuing concern.[1] One no longer hears in *Axe Handles* the same urgency expressed in *Turtle Island;* one does hear, more emphatically, the concern with cultural practice in a specific place in terms of family, community, and region.

Teaching, as a form of acting in the world, also takes on a more important function in Snyder's poems. One could argue that Snyder has gone beyond the feeling of apocalyptic crisis since the mid-1970s and gained a clearer sense of the long cycles of cultural and ecological change. Snyder has entered his fifties by the time he published *Axe Handles* and takes to heart in this collection the message he reports coming to him from his dead friend Lew Welch: "teach the children about the cycles."[2]

"Loops"

Part one of *Axe Handles* is titled "Loops" and comprises twenty-five poems, with the title poem placed first. As Julia Martin notes, "Snyder has frequently used the idea of 'looping back' to indicate a recursive sense of history and tradition. The metaphor implies at many levels a reconnection with origins, 'the old ways,' and a recognition of continuity with ancient tradition."[3] All this is certainly implied in the epigraph to the volume and restated without ambiguity in "Axe Handles." But to understand this poem, one needs first to consider the epigraph.

If the dedication, "This book is for San Juan Ridge," can be said to emphasize place, then the epigraph can be said to emphasize time, specifically the transmission of culture down through generations. Snyder identifies his epigraph as "a folk song from the Pin area [of China], 5th c. B.C." Rather than "high" literature, he draws on popular tradition, orally transmitted. The opening two lines indicate that the new is crafted on the basis of the old and that such transmission of knowledge requires models. This lesson is then applied to marriage, so that craft and culture, as well as the older generation, the present generation, and the one yet to come are all implicated in custom and ritual. The "go-between" identified in the epigraph is literally a marriage broker. In a broader cultural sense, one could say it is also the artist or poet who, through his or her role as a communicator, brings different people together and educates them about each other.

Robert Schultz and David Wyatt comment that "instruction is at the heart of this book, emphasized in its beginning and returned to frequently."[4] In essence, "Axe Handles" (5–6) provides a contemporary version of the epigraph's lesson, with the emphasis on generational communication. The "hatchet-head" lies dormant, awaiting a handle, until the poet's son Kai remembers it and wants to own a hatchet in imitation of his father. We could think of Kai as also being a hatchet-head, full of potential for useful labor but lacking the vehicle for translating that promise into practice. As Snyder shapes the hatchet handle, he is serving as a handle of knowledge that Kai can grab onto in order to use the hatchet properly when it comes his turn to labor. Snyder makes this point through his own recollection of Pound and the saying that Pound derived from the ancient Chinese, that when making an axe the model is close at hand. Snyder, in his youth, served as a hatchet-head in need of a handle and found the handle and the pattern to become a handle in turn in the poet Ezra Pound, the essayist Lu Ji, and the college professor Shih-hsiang Chen. At the same time, Snyder is shaping Kai so that he will also become a handle, as indicated near the end of the poem.

Snyder does not call Pound or Chen either a hatchet-head or a handle but calls each an "axe," because in their lives they joined together the potential of the head and the knowledge of the handle in poetic and educational practice. Snyder in his fifties has also become an "axe," complete in both functions as a "model" and as an instrument in the service of the "craft of culture" (6), and he appears confident that Kai will become an "axe" as well. As Katsunori Yamazato succinctly explains it, "Snyder's commitment to the wild territory and the subsequent inhabitory life leads him to understand a cycle of culture—flowing from Pound, Chen, the poet himself, and to his son Kai—in which one is both 'shaped' and 'shaping,' a cycle preserving and transmitting 'craft of culture.' "[5]

The next poem in "Loops," "For/From Lew," continues this emphasis on serving as a teacher. The poem is basically a dream vision in which Snyder's dead friend Lew Welch appears and speaks to him. The first two lines echo the song "Joe Hill," about a hero of the American Left, which Joan Baez sang at Woodstock.

Handing Down the Practice

Snyder implies by this allusion that Welch should also be seen as a hero, one who serves in this poem as a ''go-between'' attempting to marry the worlds of the living and the dead. Welch instructs Snyder in his responsibilities as a poet in the 1980s: ''teach the children about the cycles'' (7), i.e, the cycles of all entities on the planet, which would necessarily include teaching them about death as well as life.

''River in the Valley'' (8–9) embodies the practicing of this task in Snyder's role as a teacher to his sons.[6] The poem also shows the fine attention to specific details that recurs throughout *Axe Handles*. The first stanza establishes a set of relationships: through numerical difference, between the human ''we'' and the ''thousands of swallows''; by means of an abandoned ''overhead / roadway,'' between the humans who have created but cannot utilize it and the swallows who are able to adapt it to their own purposes; and through the solid-fluid dichotomy, between the river/creek of flowing water and the road/bridge of seemingly static concrete. The next section treats the behavior of the three humans in the presence of the nesting swallows. Gen imitates the flock's swirling flight, while Kai focuses on tracking a single bird. Their games mimic the two simultaneous forms of energy: wave and particle, as well as two different types of hunting. Meanwhile, the swallows' flight mimics the action of fish, as they flow in and out under the bridge. And as for Snyder? He is busy removing grass seeds that have stuck to his socks. As the swallows engage in a pattern replicated elsewhere in nature, so too the humans participate in such patterns, linking animal and human together. Even Snyder unwittingly finds himself participating in wild seed dispersal. This action duplicates his function as father and provides him with the same role as numerous other animals, such as bears and birds, who contribute to the flourishing of plant life.

As the three of them move on, from the abandoned causeway through the town of Colusa and out toward the mountains,

One boy asks, ''where do rivers start?''

in threads in hills, and gather down to here—
but the river
is all of it everywhere,
all flowing at once,
all one place. (9)

The conclusion of the poem begins like a factual answer but leaps quickly into metaphysics. The cycles of planetary life are treated as ''One'' cycle, just as it is ''One boy'' who speaks rather than a named individual. Snyder moves out from the particular to the universal, and a qualitative change occurs at the point at which ''threads'' of water coalesce to form a river, and the river itself comprises a whole more than the volume of individual molecules, more than the sum of its parts. Like the river, the world does not consist of isolated locations, independent atoms, but is ''all flowing at once.''

The sophistication of this poem arises not just from the philosophical complexity of its conclusion but also from the form of the poem, which is structured to replicate the phases of that final stanza. The beginning of ''River in the Valley'' consists of details and questions, perception without understanding. The second section depicts a deepening of perception through identification of humanity and nature. The third enlarges the context of the poem in terms of both land and community. The fourth fills out the rest of the watershed and provides the people with the vision necessary to encompass the entire land of which they comprise an integral part. As Yamazato observes in regard to the poem's conclusion: ''this is the kind of answer that comes from an inhabitory poet who has deeply meditated on 'the whole network,' or 'Gaia,' always focusing his attention on 'the Whole Self.' He rejects the prevalent dissecting mode of knowledge, and instead teaches the sons (and the readers) to see the interpenetrating whole—'all one place.' ''[7]

Handing Down the Practice

Several other poems in "Loops" need to be discussed briefly before turning to the next section of *Axe Handles*. "Berry Territory" (12–13) results from Snyder's friendship with Wendell Berry, another ecologically focused writer. Unlike Snyder, Berry makes his home in Kentucky and writes out of a Southern Protestant agrarian background and ethics. Snyder, in effect, pays tribute to the differences between them and their territories and to the ways in which Berry has sought to integrate himself with this particular place, much like the tortoise of the first stanza. "Changing Diapers" (18) is a send-up of the "macho" stereotype of what it means to be a "real man" in American culture. The two poems emphasize very different types of relationships. "Berry Territory" comments on the importance of continent-wide networks and sharing mutual concerns while retaining differences appropriate to one's own locale. "Changing Diapers" focuses on family and the ways in which familial duties cut across cultures.

"Painting the North San Juan School" (21–22) turns from the humor of the previously mentioned poems back to the kind of teaching called for in "For/From Lew." "Painting" focuses on community while maintaining attention on generational responsibility for handing down the culture. Even as Snyder describes the painting of the school house he manages to engage in teaching the readers about the knowledge the Ridge community has and shares. This knowledge the adult members of the community intend to teach their children in the face of the opposing values found in mainstream American culture. This conflict of values is first expressed through the juxtaposition of logging trucks that shake the school in the first stanza with the local practices of grafting, planting, and growing trees in the next one. Snyder then expresses the conflict through the contradictions between a bioregional sense of history that includes the original inhabitants of the area and one based exclusively on the practices of the ruling culture of only the past three centuries. The fragility of what the Ridge community is attempting to do is suggested by the poem's closing image: "Ladders resting on the shaky porch."

Clearly, many of these poems can be understood in terms of "loops," historical, generational, cultural, and regional. Woody Rehanek suggests that "Soy Sauce" addresses another type: "man identifying with, representing, and finally *becoming* a totem animal. This experience transcends intellectual rapport and becomes a total affinity with the nonhuman. . . . A vital aspect of shamanism is this ability to become one with the animal."[8] While "Soy Sauce," then, focuses on the human-animal relationship, it also includes Snyder's looping back to Japan, invoking a strong memory of his life there even after his years away. "Delicate Crisscrossing Beetle Trails Left in the Sand" is written from the experience of his family's visit there in 1981. Here the loop is completely literal rather than metaphoric in that the village where Masa takes her husband is a place he has visited years before meeting her. While his "trails" do indeed criss-cross, the question remains as to their purpose. But as Yamazato suggests, means and ends, experiences and purposes, are equally interpenetrating and impermanent: "From a Buddhist-ecologist view, all that is endowed with life is engaged in impermanent activities, travelling, as it were, on a dusty road to the final dispersal into the permanent cycles of things in this universe."[9]

Two poems in this section return to an image first presented in *Turtle Island:* military jets screaming through the sky. "Fishing Catching Nothing off the Breakwater near the Airport, Naha Harbor, Okinawa" (35) is set on that Japanese island, home to several U.S. military bases. "Strategic Air Command" (37), as the signature line indicates, was written in the Sierra Nevada. At the end of "What Happened Here Before" in *Turtle Island,* Snyder posed the challenge "We shall see who knows how to be." Here in "Fishing Catching Nothing" he seems to be comparing the activity of the practice flight of the jets with the unsuccessful fishing, which both criticizes militarism and places it in perspective. The second poem, "Strategic Air Command," concludes that the land is enduring while militarism is transitory, since it "Belongs to the twentieth century and its wars." In both instances, the observers are implicitly presented as superior to what is being observed because they have the proper perspective from which to evaluate the other's place.

Schultz and Wyatt argue that "True Night" (44–45) is the strongest poem in all of *Axe Handles* and several other critics concur. According to them, it "beautifully captures the tension between the urge to be out and away and the need to settle and stay"; Yamazato believes that "this is one of the best poems in *Axe Handles,* depicting Snyder's directions and life's commitment to a place."[10] The poem begins, like "River in the Valley," with a narrative of simple events: Snyder awakened from sleep chases two raccoons out of his kitchen. But suddenly the poet, Antaeus-like with bare feet touching the gravel, is transformed into a figure epitomizing millennia of human-animal interaction, and the world pours into him: "I am all alive to the night." The next stanza records his observations of that night, followed by his return to the house. Here the meditational part of the poem begins as he identifies himself with dandelions and sea anemones who have also opened themselves to the world. His sleeping family, however, draws him back from this totemic immersion as he ruefully concludes that a person cannot stay awake for too long in such darkness. At this point, "True Night" is strongly reminiscent of "The Bed in the Sky" in *Regarding Wave.* There too the poet was tempted by the solitary experiencing of the night but elected to return to his lover's bed.

After this turning point, Snyder speaks of the sleep he needs to prepare for "the waking that comes" with each new dawn. The reader can understand this waking in several ways. One, in the light of day his connections to the rest of humanity are more self-evident; two, there is the waking to responsibilities that he must renew as a member of his community; three, there is the sense of his obligation to the future, to the "dawn" of that better culture he is attempting to assist into being. To remain in the dark too long, to be carried away permanently into the wilderness of the land and of his own mind, would be to renege on the various promises he has made in his life and his poetry. One of those promises is to reverence Gaia, which Snyder has defined elsewhere as "the whole network."[11]

"Little Songs for Gaia"

The "Little Songs for Gaia" section works best when read as a single unit. In fact, Snyder published it in 1979 as a Copper Canyon Press chapbook. This section is, as Schultz and Wyatt note, "made of glimpses—heightened moments of perception or feeling communicating an intimacy of contact with things which spices and sustains the life of the poet."[12] And Martin provides a cogent argument for its being placed in the middle of *Axe Handles,* even though it was written prior to a number of the poems that precede it: "a net is made of loops, while it is mythically the work of the goddess to weave the disparate threads of the net or web together."[13] Snyder's concept of Gaia is based on both the Gaia hypothesis that he discusses in *The Old Ways* and the Buddhist-Avatamsaka notion of Indra's jeweled net and the interpenetration and co-origination of all aspects of the universe. When Snyder invokes the term Gaia he also invokes a sense of spirituality and religious awe that philosophical and scientific terms lack. If all aspects of Gaia are alive and co-originating, then Gaia too must be living, and each experience of this entity provides access to its total mystery.

This sense of religious awe permeates the "Little Songs" section as instanced by the opening lines in which Snyder observes and meditates on the wonders of the particularities of San Francisco Bay, which is a "slow-paced / system" within other systems (49). Part of his awe is induced by the recognition that the area's time frame far exceeds the abilities of human consciousness to comprehend it. This difference in time frames and perception is reiterated throughout the section, perhaps most eloquently when Snyder compares the relationships of crickets to humans, with humans to trees, with trees "to the rocks and the hills" (51). Each is living at its own pace. This set of ratios is immediately followed by "Corn Maidens," a dream vision poem similar to "For/From Lew" that heightens the sense of spirituality, here in terms of the Native American shamanist symbol identified in the title. At the end of "Little Songs," Snyder addresses Gaia directly as the owner of a house he has broken into seeking wisdom in "the library." He writes to apologize for the mess he made while there but in effect is offering an apology for all of humanity's despoliation and degradation of Earth's environment.

While Snyder wields Gaia imagery with sincerity, humility, and reverence, there remains the problem of sex-typing the planet through the use of such mythic symbols.[14] Martin highlights this difficulty: "As metaphor, Gaia represents a perspective that is clearly of a higher logical type than those which either welcome or bemoan an identification of the 'feminine' with 'nature,' and represent the goddess as the reverse image of the 'masculine,' 'patriarchal' god." Nevertheless, the dangers of sexism and the continued identification of woman and nature that has meant the degradation of both in Western cultures remains a problem. In terms of Snyder's use, Martin notes that "although I do find Gaia an effective metaphor, I think that the poetry shows very little self criticism on this subject, and little sense of the problems inherent in making such connections."[15] Elsewhere Snyder has shown some sense of this problem, particularly in his championing of gender equality among American Buddhists and in his response to Sherman Paul's study of his poetry. There he states: "Remove the question of gender. . . . 'Patriarchal values' are values of hierarchy, domination, and centralization."[16]

"Nets"

If the first part of *Axe Handles* deploys twenty-five poems to establish a set of thematic loops, then the third part, according to Martin, uses another twenty-six poems to weave those loops into four nets of relationships. Other critics would seem to assent to this argument when they claim that ''Nets'' treats political, cultural, social, and ecological networks. Rehanek concurs with this orientation, but takes it a step further in terms of analyzing the reason for the section's subdivisions: ''The four parts of 'Nets' are roughly equivalent to four layers of healing songs defined in 'Poetry, Community & Climax,' the final chapter of *The Real Work*.'' He goes on to define these as: one, unity with nature; two, humanity with others outside one's own group; three, speaking as a voice for the unconscious; four, treating a state of mind analogous to the ''climax'' condition of forests, which Snyder has clearly defined in *Turtle Island*.[17]

As in the ''Little Songs'' section, in ''Nets I'' the reader finds several poems focused almost entirely on specific details that remind the poet of the spiritual presence of Gaia. In the first poem, ''Walked Two Days in Snow, Then It Cleared for Five'' (63–64), this becomes apparent when Snyder shifts from the description of different animals sharing the land through which he is walking to direct address in the final line. ''Geese Gone Beyond'' (65–66) continues in this vein by treating the hunting of geese as an action deserving the respect of ritual behavior. Snyder indicates such behavior in the third stanza by explaining that he is kneeling in the bow of the canoe, and then he identifies his kneeling with that practiced in Japanese ceremonies. The last line of the poem, ''The one who is the first to feel to go,'' implies that the animals are participants in the ritual of hunting to gather food, along the lines of the kind of ''hunting magic'' discussed in *Earth House Hold*.

The most sacred moment of ''Nets I'' comes with the poem ''24:IV:40075, 3:30 PM, n. of Coaldale, Nevada, A Glimpse through a Break in the Storm of the Summit of the White Mountains'' (71). The title, which has more words in it than the rest of the poem, establishes with absolute precision the moment, place, and cause for the composition of this prayer to Gaia. The poem can be analyzed formally and appreciated for the mastery of its technique, but it is more appropriate to respect the religious sensibility with which Snyder has imbued it by means of a meditative reading rather than a formal explication.

If ''Nets I'' engages the sacred, then clearly ''Nets II'' engages the profane world of political and cultural ideologies. ''The Grand Entry'' (77–78) takes a critical but whimsical look at the attachment of national allegiance to the rodeo. The next several poems treat Snyder's experience of serving on the California Arts Council and his friendship with the governor at that time, Jerry Brown. ''What Have I Learned'' (85) returns Snyder to the basic point introduced at the beginning of the volume, as he concludes that when a person gets something right ''you pass it on.''

''Nets III'' finds Snyder writing about the place where he lives, San Juan Ridge, and Alaska and the Australian outback, which he has visited in order to learn from the native peoples and more recent inhabitants. The two poems on Alaska are, interestingly enough, sandwiched between two poems from the Ridge that focus on tools. The first, ''A Maul for Bill and Cindy's Wedding'' (89), speaks of the proper handling of the tool, letting oneself go with the flow and momentum of the maul, and the way in which, if handled properly, it will cleanly split wood. Marriage may also be seen as a tool—cultural rather than physical—because its function when properly wielded is to join together what is separate and distinct. The second, ''Removing the Plate of the Pump on the Hydraulic System of the Backhoe'' (93), shows Snyder appreciating a high-technology machine. Here he consciously writes against the naive view that some of his readers have that to learn to live the ''old ways'' means to forsake all technology. Instead, Snyder repeatedly emphasizes the idea of *appropriate* technology, such as the solar cells that power his computer. In this poem the final lines about the "relentless clarity" that constitutes the "heart" of labor suggest the true focus of one's attention when approaching technology and the equipment it has produced.

"Alaska" (90) and "Dillingham, Alaska, the Willow Tree Bar" (91–92), then, are placed within the context of work on the Ridge. In the first poem, Snyder joins others in looking at the Alaskan pipeline and a graffito that has been spraypainted on it: "Where will it all end?" Snyder knows that he shares the concern of the anonymous author, but also that he is complicitous to some extent with that which he opposes. The next stanza begins with "drive back," and the following stanza begins "And then fly on." For Snyder to participate in efforts to determine appropriate human inhabitation of Alaska, including working its minerals and metals, he must utilize one of the products that constantly threatens Alaska's ecosystem: oil. The final line suggests that he has not resolved this dilemma but continues working through it. The second poem addresses complicity again, but in a more overtly critical fashion, and is reminiscent of "Dusty Braces" in *Turtle Island*. Snyder is among the oil workers in a bar, and he notes the ways in which these men are subjected to the totalizing sameness of identically designed franchise operations found around the world. Such businesses ignore the differences and particularities of bioregions, ecosystems, and human cultures in their constant expansion for profit. At poem's end, Snyder makes clear that he is primarily angry at, and condemning, the economic system that compels these men to labor, not at the men themselves.

Snyder ends "Nets III" with the longest poem in the volume, "Uluru Wild Fig Song" (95–98), which upholds the integrity of the "old ways" of inhabiting the world as practiced by the natives of Australia. Through the primitive practices he portrays, Snyder is able to return from the profane world of politics and capitalist economics to the sacred world of interpenetration of human and nature. And through the rituals outlined in shadowy detail and the central image of the wild fig, Snyder encourages readers to recognize that this interpenetration has to occur on both the conscious and unconscious levels, the cultivated and the wild parts of both nature and mind.

"Nets IV" includes a mixture of poems, playful and serious, that circle around the themes raised earlier in the volume. In "Money Goes Upstream" (101–102) Snyder reaffirms his conviction that the current state of culture is a short-lived aberration and that the power into which he has tapped will endure. The experiences recorded in "Uluru Wild Fig Song" enable him to maintain his optimism and his grounding even when he is trapped in boring meetings held in sterile buildings. As Schultz and Wyatt see it, "against this insidious influence Snyder poses his own ability to summon the corrective presence of nature. . . . This power is twofold: Snyder's firsthand knowledge of nature . . . and his ability to summon what is not present keeps him ever close to the natural law from which he borrows his authority."[18] Several poems address the reality of violence, decay, and death in the natural as well as the civilized world. And in the case of "The Canyon Wren" (111), Snyder records a last experience of a part of nature that has literally been submerged by human engineering—in this case, the construction of a reservoir. The song of the wren will remain, Snyder contends, "To purify our ears." It will inspire him to continue to build a different culture here on Turtle Island, one that will not drown the wren for the sake of another reservoir.

Readers will respond extremely differently to Snyder's last poem in *Axe Handles* depending on their overall attitude toward the way of life and the beliefs that he has espoused in the previous poems. The first half of this work, like many of the other poems, relishes the beauty of the everyday details of "fording a stream" and listening to its music and the parallel music inside the speaker's body. Part two is a parody of the United States national anthem. Snyder pledges allegiance not to the United States but to Turtle Island, not to a government but to an ecosystem. And in the final line, "With joyful interpenetration for all," he clarifies the title,

"For All." Unlike national anthems, which focus on governments and peoples, Snyder's poem focuses on an ecosystem and all its inhabitants, including people, animals, plants, and spirits.

Certainly, as Molesworth claims, *Axe Handles* continues and extends the concerns of *Turtle Island* and confronts the same problems and evils, but it is quite a different book and frequently exhibits a different kind of poetry. Those readers who were looking for the militancy of *Turtle Island* were no doubt disappointed. Those looking for formal innovation may or may not have appreciated the sophistication of much of Snyder's apparent simplicity. Andrew Schelling, in comparing various critics' castigation of *Axe Handles* for its popularity (it sold 30,000 copies in six months, a phenomenal figure for a book of poems), draws this conclusion: "As he defers to an audience more interested in botany and politics than literature, Snyder has introduced numerous explanatory digressions—a practice poetically suspect to those who have cut their teeth on Modernist texts, but indisputably useful for the retention and transmission of certain sorts of information. It is actually an ancient practice."[19]

Left Out in the Rain

In 1986 Snyder published another poetry volume with North Point Press, a book unlike any other he had produced before. *Left Out in the Rain: New Poems 1947–1985* brings together poems that Snyder had written over his entire poetic career but had never previously included in a book or chapbook. The reasons for their exclusion are many, including concerns over quality and seriousness. While *Left Out in the Rain* contains some excellent and interesting poems, it is unlikely that this volume will gain as much attention as any of the others he has published to date. Rather, it will be read primarily by those already familiar with Snyder's work who

want to fill in gaps, read comprehensively, learn more about Snyder's biography, or study the development of his poetics.

If one has already read Snyder's other volumes, echoes of those
poems reverberate throughout *Left Out in the Rain*. But it is important to remember that the poems of this recent collection often
came first. Many of them are examples of poetic experiments more
successfully realized elsewhere. As Jack Hicks claims, based on
conversations with Snyder, the poet's "intent was to bring the
early poems into print faithful to the original texts, with little
revision."[20] The first two poems were written when Snyder was
seventeen and the most recent when he was fifty-three. The volume contains, then, 154 poems written over a forty-year time
span.

The first two poems, "Elk Trails" and " 'Out of the Soil and
Rock,' " which comprise the "Introduction" to the volume, are
informative in terms of the clarity of Snyder's position on nature
versus the city at an early age.[21] Snyder displays in the first poem
a more heightened sensitivity to ecology and spirituality than one
might anticipate. In "Elk Trails" he defines "Instinct" as the
"ancient, coarse-haired, / Thin-flanked God" of these trails,
which is to say a consciousness that is not rational or logical but is
also not ignorant. He also displays a recognition that understanding
and following the trails is not the same as finding or becoming the
Elk. While "Elk Trails" is set in a mountain wilderness, " 'Out of
the Soil and Rock' " is set in the city. The youthful, western,
wilderness-oriented Snyder optimistically dismisses the apparent
solidity of New York City as an illusion of permanence when contrasted with the web of natural generation that he outlines.

Part two consists of nineteen poems written while Snyder was
attending Reed College. Most of these appear to be exercises in
preparation for writing *Myths & Texts,* particularly the poems that
treat shamanism, such as "Message from Outside" (15) and
"Birth of the Shaman" (19). Ten of these belong to a sequence
titled "Atthis" about a love affair, showing Snyder's desire to

work in sequential and extended poetic forms. Most are relatively weak, with the the best poem the last one, "Seaman's Ditty" (30–31), written in a sing-song rhythm. Part three comprises another seventeen poems from the years between college and Japan. Some of these would have been written at the same time as the early *Riprap* poems. Obvious here is the influence of other poets from whom Snyder was learning his craft, such as Walt Whitman, Ezra Pound, and Robinson Jeffers. Also, the cultural influences of Native American tribes, Japanese literature, and Hindu myths begin to appear. From the viewpoint of Snyder's biography, "Makings" (56) is the most interesting. Snyder reflects on his Depression childhood and then observes that he has chosen in the prosperous 1950s to maintain a life of poverty because it provides a certain freedom.

Part four contains fourteen poems from the first years in Japan and the time he spent working on the *Sappa Creek*. "Bomb Test" (63) reveals his continuing concern with nuclear proliferation, while "Dullness in February: Japan" (64–65) expresses his skepticism about the sincerity of Japanese Buddhists. Yamazato points out that this is the first poem that Snyder has published in which he explicitly registers that skepticism.[22] More significant, though, is his clear intent at poem's end to hold on to his own commitment to Zen and to practice it as a wandering monk in the United States. While some of these poems could certainly have been added to *Riprap,* they would not have altered that volume in any significant way.

Part five covers the ten-year period from his second return to Japan until he, Masa, and Kai came to settle in California. "Three Poems for Joanne" (91–93) are the most interesting in this section, along with "Crash" (97–98). The first of "Three Poems" is titled "Loving Words" and seems to record an early moment in Kyger and Snyder's relationship, emphasizing their mutual commitment to poetry and a strong sense of optimism. The second, "The Heart of the Wood," records Snyder's belief in the intensity and depth of their love. The third, "Joanne My Wife," abruptly depicts the decay of their relationship. The reversal in tone here raises doubts about the accuracy of the previous two poems. In "Joanne My Wife," the depiction is realistic rather than idealized; and it comes as no surprise that the optimism is gone.

In "Crash," Snyder recounts having an accident in which he collided on his motorcycle with a Japanese man on a bicycle. The strength of this poem comes from the way Snyder focuses on the relationship between mind and body, consciousness and behavior. The fifth line reveals that he is "distracted or intense"; by the twenty-second line he wonders "Where was my mind"; and, by the thirtieth line, in meditation at the temple, he recognizes the potentially disastrous consequences of "my inattention." The poem shifts from a description of events to a meditation on the importance of "attention" to one's own actions in the world.

Part six, "Shasta Nation," comprises thirty-three poems written during the same years that he was putting together *Regarding Wave, Turtle Island,* and *Axe Handles,* and two years beyond that. The most interesting poems here are "Burned Out," " 'The Trail Is Not a Trail,' " "We Make Our Vows Together With All Beings," and "The Persimmons." "The Persimmons," which was written while on a visit to China in 1983, is perhaps the most fascinating of these since it exposes the superficiality of the exotic that too often distracts people from the profundity of the ordinary. The occasion of the poem is an excursion to the Great Wall and the Ming tombs, but along the way Snyder notices the bountiful harvest of persimmons, a fruit which predates any of the Chinese empires. As a result, the persimmon becomes a far more significant symbol than the ones he has been brought to see. While the tombs tell of kings who, even after death, consumed the fruits of the peasants' labor, the persimmons tell of a far greater historical continuity: "the people and trees that prevail" (151).[23]

Parts seven and eight of *Left Out in the Rain* present a set of very brief poems and a set of humorous prose pieces respectively.

In the last section two items stand out. The first is "Sestina of the End of the Kalpa" (187–88), which exemplifies the outrageously inappropriate fusion of a highly formalized European poetic structure and an Eastern theme of the world's destruction and thereby succeeds in carnivalizing apocalypse. The second ends the volume. Snyder closes *Left Out in the Rain* with a humorous tale titled "Coyote Man, Mr. President, & the Gunfighters," which is one of Snyder's first formal contributions to the reviving art of American storytelling. This tale is based on a third-century B.C. Chinese story by the Daoist Chuang-tzu, but the characters are drawn from Native American and cowboy traditions and applied to contemporary national politics. Snyder calls for an end to militarism and centralized governments. In concluding his 1987 study of Snyder, Yamazato makes a general statement that seems pertinent to ending an overview of *Left Out in the Rain:* "The problem of civilization remains the central issue in the poet's thinking, and his future poetic efforts will continue to address this problem."[24]

Notes

1. Charles Molesworth, "Getting a Handle on It," *American Book Review* 6.5–6 (1984) 15.

2. Gary Snyder, *Axe Handles* (San Francisco: North Point Press, 1983) 7. Further quotations from this volume are cited in the text.

3. Julia Martin, "The Pattern which Connects: Metaphor in Gary Snyder's Later Poetry," *Western American Literature* 22 (1987); rpt. in *Critical Essays on Gary Snyder,* ed. Patrick D. Murphy (Boston: G. K. Hall, 1990) 199.

4. Robert Schultz and David Wyatt, "Gary Snyder and the Curve of Return," *Virginia Quarterly Review* 62 (1986); rpt. in Murphy 161.

5. Katsunori Yamazato, "Seeking a Fulcrum: Gary Snyder and Japan (156-1975)," Ph.D. dissertation, University of California, Davis, 1987, 168. See Tim Dean, *Gary Snyder and the American Unconscious: Inhabiting the Ground* (New York: St. Martin's, 1991) 145–52, for a different, Lacanian reading of this poem.

6. Portions of this interpretation are based on my note "Gary Snyder's Endless River," *NMAL* 9.1 (1985) Item 4.

7. Yamazato 169.

8. Woody Rehanek, "The Shaman Songs of Gary Snyder," *Okanogan Natural News* No.19 (Summer 1984) 9.

9. Yamazato 177.

10. Schultz and Wyatt 157; Yamazato 173.

11. Yamazato 166; he cites Snyder's defining Gaia in this way in the essay "Good, Wild, Sacred," which appeared in *CoEvoluton Quarterly* about the time *Axe Handles* was published and was reprinted in *The Practice of the Wild.*

12. Schultz and Wyatt 164.

13. Martin 203.

14. See my essay, "Sex-Typing the Planet: Gaia Imagery and the Problem of Subverting Patriarchy," *Environmental Ethics* 10 (1988): 155–68.

15. Martin 206.

16. Snyder's response to Paul's remarks is included in Sherman Paul, *In Search of the Primitive: Rereading David Antin, Jerome Rothenberg, and Gary Snyder* (Baton Rouge: Louisiana State University Press, 1986) 299.

17. Rehanek 11–12.

18. Schultz and Wyatt 162.

19. Andrew Schelling, "How the Grinch Imitated Gary Snyder," *Sulfur* No.13 (1985) 160.

20. Jack Hicks, "Poetic Composting in Gary Snyder's *Left Out in the Rain,*" in Murphy 250.

21. Gary Snyder, *Left Out in the Rain: New Poems 1947–1985* (San Francisco: North Point Press, 1986) 5–8. Further references to this edition are given in the text.

22. Yamazato 189.

23. See Scott McLean, " 'Thirty Miles of Dust: There Is No Other Life,' " in *Gary Snyder: Dimensions of a Life,* ed. Jon Halper (San Francisco: Sierra Club Books, 1991) 137–38.

24. Yamazato 200.

CHAPTER EIGHT

Of Wildness and Wilderness in Plain Language: *The Practice of the Wild*

Since the publication of *Axe Handles* Snyder has continued to address the central problem of civilization but in a more diversified way. He has written poetry, given poetry readings, written prose, and begun teaching as a permanent member of a university faculty. His latest published volume is a work qualitatively superior and more significant than any other prose volume he has published. *The Practice of the Wild* is a sophisticated yet clear, complex yet uncomplicated, unified book about *knowing how to be* in this world. In one of the early reviews of this book, Ray Olson claims that Snyder's essays "constitute the finest wisdom (and also ecological) literature of our time."[1]

Earth House Hold has been his only prose volume treated critically in its own right and remains the prose most often quoted, with perhaps the exception of the essay "Four Changes" at the end of *Turtle Island*. Yet *Earth House Hold* is not a unified work but a selection of discrete pieces that work together because of the life and mind behind them; a full appreciation of this collection is to some extent dependent on the reader's knowledge of Snyder's poetry. *The Practice of the Wild* functions on a different level of organization, being thematically unified by a discussion of the interrelationships of the meanings of freedom and responsibility, wilderness and wildness, humanity and nature, mind and body, conscious and unconscious, and knowledge and action.

It has been inaccurately defined as "nature writing," compared time and again with Thoreau's *Walden,* and discussed in terms of primitivism and nostalgia. But the Anglo-American tradition of nature writing has tended to be based on a sense of the author's alienation and distance from the natural world and a male desire to be reunited with something felt to be missing or lost. Thoreau had to leave Concord and go to the woods to try his two-year experiment of simple living by Walden Pond and in so doing embodied the romantic notions of human alienation from nature and nostalgic yearning to return to some Edenic ideal.

Snyder is concerned instead with people conducting practice in place. As he remarked in an interview with David Robertson conducted while Snyder was completing *The Practice of the Wild,* "I hope that the book I am now writing will be stimulating to a broad range of people and provide them with historical, ecological, and personal visions all at the same time. I would like to see the book be political in the sense of helping people shape the way they want to live and act in the world."[2]

The Practice of the Wild leaps beyond the traditional limitations of the genre of nature writing. This is ecological writing in its fullest sense and treats in detail ideas that Snyder could only present in outline in his poems. And while the volume is optimistic, it is not idealistic in the sense of being utopian or naive. Robertson's comment to Snyder is pertinent here: "One of the things I like so much about your prose writing is your ability to lay out a vision of life as it ought to be, at the same time recognizing very hard-headedly that actual life is rooted in ambiguity and frustration over uncompleted goals."[3] Robertson may in part be responding to Snyder's recognition reiterated since the early 1970s, first to Ekbert Faas and then to numerous other interviewers including Robertson, that "we are entering into a really critical age. Things are bad and they are going to get worse."[4] But, as Snyder maintains throughout *The Practice of the Wild,* he also knows that they can get better.

"The Etiquette of Freedom"

The first section of *The Practice of the Wild,* "The Etiquette of Freedom," begins with the notion of a "compact" as one of the forms of proper relationships among all entities who inhabit this earth. Snyder realistically recognizes that these arrangements include predatory as well as symbiotic, mutually beneficial ones. In what humans consider the wild reaches of the world, nonhuman creatures work out their lives in relationships that are conditioned first and foremost by the various food chains of their bioregions. To date, as Snyder points out, contemporary humans are the worst example of creatures disrupting their own and other creatures' food chains. To counter this process Snyder emphasizes the need to educate people so that they will work to cease "causing unnecessary harm" to other beings as well as to themselves.[5]

From the notion of "compact," Snyder moves to an investigation of the popular American dream of "wild and free" and describes that dream in terms of a freedom that is achieved only when people recognize the real conditions of existence in which they participate. A crucial component of those conditions is "impermanence," which Americans in particular seem to fear, given their attitudes toward aging and dying. To realize freedom, Snyder argues, people are going to have to begin to build a civilization that can come to terms with and sustain "wildness." Suspecting that his readers do not have a very good sense of such terms as "Nature, Wild, *and* Wilderness" (8), Snyder elaborates the derivations and definitional developments of these three words.

What people have for centuries termed the "wild" is that which has an ecosystem sufficiently flexible that humans who have not previously participated in it may enter it and survive. In contrast, contemporary cities are so inflexible and closed that wild vegetation and animals haven't a chance and generally rarely venture in. It is important to remember, however, that human beings at various historical moments developed within and as functioning parts of wild ecosystems.

Snyder then relates language to body, swerving around the popular Western tendency to separate mind and body or to perceive them as in contradiction with one another. He points out that "language is a mind-body system that coevolved with our needs and nerves" (17); i.e., it is psychic *and* physical, since the psyche is part of the body. And poetry enters the picture as one of the ways in which language can serve the re-education of human beings to their own wild origins.

"The Place, the Region, and the Commons"

Having developed the idea of wild ecosystems and the wildness that must be reasserted along with recovering wilderness, Snyder turns his attention to conceptions of place. He emphasizes here the ways in which peoples relate to the land by means of an understanding of locale, region, and community. He begins with a position shared by Wendell Berry and numerous Native Americans: non-Native Americans are a set of rootless, un-placed and displaced peoples, and this condition is fundamentally unhealthy; it produces dis-ease. Snyder starts with a concept of home as hearth and moves to an understanding of region based on local specifics and on one's apprehension of that region as a living, interactive place, not a national or governmental abstraction composed of dotted lines on a distorted map.

The "commons" is a European practice of setting aside land for communal activities, and Snyder applies this idea to the sharing of "natural areas." Various forms of commons can be found around the world, including in Japanese farming villages. In the United States, commons were a rare feature of the East but did turn up in the West, due to climate and topography, and have been developed perhaps most fully in relationship to equitable access to water. Snyder believes that it is absolutely necessary to return to a system of commons and that this system needs to be used worldwide and should be extended to include such aspects of the biosphere as the air and the oceans. On the land, Snyder thinks that the greatest hope for recovering the commons lies in instituting localized bioregional governments and community practices. Fundamentally, "bioregionalism is the entry of place into the dialectic of history. Also we might say that there are 'classes' which have so far been overlooked—the animals, rivers, rocks, and grasses—now entering history" (41). Snyder renders these claims concrete by relating the way he and others who inhabit San Juan Ridge are learning their place and their role in that place.

"Tawny Grammar"

In this section of *The Practice of the Wild* Snyder turns his attention to manifestations of bioregional practice in terms of the cultural specifics of peoples and what the healthier cultures have in common. He draws on his experiences in Asia as well as North America to develop his points. In Alaska, Snyder finds significant parallels between the means by which the Inupiaq are attempting to raise their children and the practices of the San Juan Ridge school back home. One of the issues that Snyder discusses here is the relationship between oral transmissions and written transmissions of cultures. In a literate society, he notes, "books are our grandparents" (61), because in oral cultures it is the elders who transmit the cultural lore and values by means of stories.

Such considerations lead Snyder into meditations on nature writing, nature as a book, and an ecology of language. Snyder claims that grammars, like metaphors, are ways of interpreting reality, and that "tawny grammars" come from nature itself in its myriad manifestations. Snyder's point is not so much to argue for the organic and evolutionary character of language as to deflate the homocentric egotism of those who like to imagine "language as a uniquely human gift" (77).

"Good, Wild, Sacred"

Tom Clark, writing about *The Practice of the Wild* as a whole, claims that "the essays are deployed poetically, less like steps in an argument than as spokes radiating around a single, urgent, central theme: the need for re-establishing those traditional practices of wilderness that once linked humanity in a single, harmonic chord with the animals, plants, lands and water."[6] "Good, Wild, Sacred" can be seen as being structured in the same way. Snyder begins with this triad of key concepts, centered on "wild," and works through a series of reflections on historical and present-day experience. He speaks of the contradiction within an "agrarian theology" that holds that humans render themselves more holy by "weeding out" the wild from their own nature, at the same time that their having done the same to cattle and pigs has altered those animals from "intelligent and alert in the wild into sluggish meat-making machines" (79). In the process of attempting to elevate themselves, humans have degraded nature and reduced natural intelligence. Snyder necessarily rejects any theology based on a separation of the physical and the spiritual and speaks approvingly here of Native American beliefs that connect land and spirit.

From the spiritual practices of North America's inhabitory peoples, Snyder then turns to what he has learned about spirit and place from the aboriginal people of Australia. In particular, he focuses on the ways in which their stories about themselves as people are intimately tied to the land in which they live. In that land exist certain sacred places, some of which he was privileged to visit. He was told that some of those places were defined as "teaching spots" and some as "dreaming spots." This experience prompts him to meditate on "dreamtime," which he believes "is the mode of the eternal moment of creating, of being, as contrasted with the mode of cause and effect in time" (84). Differentiating between the linear time frame that dominates Western thought and the dream time of aboriginal peoples leads Snyder to think of Buddhism, particularly the Avatamsaka Sutra, and the practices of Japan's aboriginal people, the Ainu. Snyder reflects sadly on the fact that in present-day Japan so little of the Ainu and Shinto practices in relation to the sacredness of land remain.

Toward the end of the essay, Snyder circles back to the North American present and eventually to the land in which he lives, where the essay started. He makes an extremely important point that runs counter to much of European and American thinking that has been current for centuries: "It is not nature-as-chaos which threatens us, but the State's presumption that *it* has created order" (92); and, further, "Nature is orderly. That which appears to be chaotic in nature is only a more complex kind of order" (93).

"Blue Mountains Constantly Walking"

The essay "Blue Mountains Constantly Walking" is heavily dependent for its meaning on Snyder's deep and abiding philosophical, spiritual, and aesthetic debts to Japan and Buddhism. Snyder begins the essay by talking about Dogen, the thirteenth-century Buddhist monk, and his "Mountains and Waters Sutra," delivered in 1240. He then links Dogen's attention to mountains to the practices of Buddhist pilgrimages and attitudes about sacred mountains, such as Mt. Hiei.

Snyder not only provides historical information about such pilgrimages but also includes personal experience. It is useful to remember that while Snyder was in Japan he took vows with the

Yamabushi monks, as he describes some of that initiation here. The Yamabushi are a sect of mountain ascetic monks, and Snyder reminds his reader that "in East Asia 'mountains' are often synonymous with wilderness" (100), particularly since they are the terrain impervious to wilderness-destroying agriculture. But mountains cannot be understood properly in a vacuum, since they enter into relationship with the rest of nature. Dogen's sutra is, after all, about "mountains *and* waters," because, as Snyder observes: "mountains and rivers indeed form each other: waters are precipitated by heights, carve or deposit landforms in their flowing descent, and weight the offshore continental shelves with sediment to ultimately tilt more uplifts" (101–2). Poems in *Regarding Wave* are informed by this attitude as can be noted when Snyder remarks here that a mountain range is sometimes referred to "as a network of veins on the back of a hand" (102), an image which also appears in *Regarding Wave*. What is most important, however, is not the ability to make associations among the different aspects of nature—mountains like veins, bodies like streams; it is being able to realize that there is no *nature* as an entity but only *naturing,* a process of interaction and mutual transformation. Solidity consists of energy transformations in an apparent, but only apparent, period of stasis.

"Ancient Forests of the Far West"

According to Clark, "Ancient Forests of the Far West" comprises "the crowning component of this stirring, thoughtful field report on the tenuous state of the wild in our time."[7] Interestingly enough, Snyder uses as epigraph for this essay the same lines from Exodus that he quotes in "Logging 2" of *Myths & Texts.* Thus he explicitly loops back to poetry written nearly forty years earlier. In the opening section of the essay he loops back even farther to youthful experiences growing up and working in those Far West forests. This essay provides one of the clearest pictures Snyder has presented of the events behind the poetry of the "Logging" section of *Myths & Texts* as well as early poems, such as "The Late Snow & Lumber Strike of the Summer of Fifty-four" in *Riprap*.

Snyder uses these personal memories as a way of detailing an appropriate type of logging, selective and sensitive to the bioregion and to the individual trees that are dying. From this lesson of the right way to do things, Snyder switches to the history of U.S. forest management, as well as to an analysis of the ecological specifics of the ancient western forests. Snyder notes that "the forests of the maritime Pacific Northwest are the last remaining forests of any size left in the temperate zone" worldwide (130). And he details the history of the loss of corresponding forests in the Mediterranean and East Asia before returning to the threats that the surviving forests face from the U.S. government and its various agencies. Snyder speaks lovingly and respectfully of the forests of his own region and the need and ways to protect them. This essay ends with a determined anger in which the tasks of Snyder and reader alike are delineated: "We must make the hard-boiled point that the world's trees are virtually worth more standing than they would be as lumber, because of such diverse results of deforestation as life-destroying flooding in Bangladesh and Thailand, the extinction of millions of species of animals and plants, and global warming. . . . We are all endangered yokels" (143).

"On the Path, Off the Trail"

Paths and trails have served writers as metaphors for an entire series of human activities, both spiritual and physical, for centuries. In this essay Snyder participates in this tradition by developing his own literal and metaphoric senses of these terms. He also introduces the concept of "networks" to distinguish between two aspects of an individual's life. As Snyder sees it, community is grounded in place, while work is often grounded in associations that take one beyond place into a network of people engaged in the same or related tasks. As a result "networks cut across communities with their own kind of territoriality" (144). The problem for Snyder is that in the present day people often relate only to their network and fail to establish themselves in their community as well.

Snyder turns to Asia to develop a notion related to path and trail—that of "way," which includes the idea of path but extends it to an entire perception of being, to the realms of philosophies, religions, and ideologies. One of the ways that people travel is that of art, which Snyder discusses in terms of the relationship between tradition and creativity. This in turn brings him back to a relationship addressed at the beginning of *The Practice of the Wild,* which is that of freedom and responsibility. Manifestations of this relationship can be thought of in terms of discipline and spontaneity, as well as models and innovation. Snyder here resorts again to Buddhism and the various means by which its masters have tried to teach the relationship of the tradition, discipline, and path of Buddhist practice and individual experience—the last marked by the distinction between prescribed forms of meditation and the individual experiencing of enlightenment. Snyder concludes that "there are paths that can be followed, and there is a path that cannot—it is not a path, it is the wilderness. There is a 'going' but no goer, no destination, only the whole field" (151). And, then, he immediately departs the realm of metaphor to talk about his own experience, which led him to study Zen in Japan, as well as to return to the United States as the place to practice what he had learned. Snyder ends with a warning about the relationships of freedom and responsibility, discipline and spontaneity, tradition and innovation:

"But we need paths and trails and will always be maintaining them. You must first be on the path, before you can turn and walk into the wild" (154).

"The Woman Who Married a Bear" and "Survival and Sacrament"

In "The Woman Who Married a Bear" Snyder brings together tradition and innovation, myth and experience, with a popular Native American tale of intersexuality between humans and other animals. He begins with the mythical story. Then, rather than explaining the tale, he begins to relate the history of bears in North America. This too becomes a story as Snyder retells with more realistic details rather than mythic ones the bear-human marriage myth. Like any good myth, Snyder's story educates readers about the world, specifically about the lives of bears and their relationship to their environment. Then, with his version of the story ended, Snyder relates the source of the tale and a little information about the Native American woman who told it, followed by a suggestion of the ubiquity of bear-human stories through references to Greek mythology.

The reader may keep waiting for Snyder to analyze the story, but he never does. Instead, he ends with another story, about a Native American bear dance he witnessed in 1977. What is revealed here, rather than claimed or explained, is the power that myth can carry in the present day and the ways by which it can help bridge the gap between animal and human that, as the story of the woman who married a bear suggests, once did not exist.

"Survival and Sacrament" serves as Snyder's conclusion to *The Practice of the Wild*. It begins on an ominous note by warning of the terrifying difference between death and the "end to birth," that is, between an individual's death and the end of the coming into being of an entire species. Since their arrival in North America white human beings have been not only witnesses but also the cause of the "end to birth" of countless species at an ever-increasing rate with no conception of the suffering involved or the long range effects on the ecosystems of this continent and the entire planetary biosphere. Snyder points out that excessive human reproduction, particularly in the past three hundred years, is a crucial dimension of this problem.

Snyder opens his conclusion with a warning, but he ends it with a promise of covenant. That promise begins with the argument that a true human quest "requires embracing the other as oneself" and that a movement in the world is growing that recognizes just such a necessity (180). This necessity does not take the form of developing a more advanced civilization, as one might expect, but of developing a wilder culture, a "culture of the wilderness" (180). This phrase encapsulates a dual recognition. One, nature is always a social construct in terms of the limits of human understanding and interaction with the rest of the world; two, society is always a natural construct arising in relation to and on the basis of natural conditions of existence. Snyder closes his book with a discussion of "Grace," both as prayer and behavior, as a socially constructed natural act which recognizes that "eating is a sacrament" (184). To approach eating with respect is to recognize human integration with the rest of the world in which people live and die, and in which people cause other beings to live and die as well, either necessarily or capriciously. By this emphasis on grace Snyder has returned to the beginning of *The Practice of the Wild,* teaching his readers about a particular form of the "etiquette of freedom," one which recognizes and gratefully affirms human responsibility.

Notes

1. Ray Olson, Review of *The Practice of the Wild, Booklist* (15 September 1990) 134.

2. David Robertson, "Practicing the Wild—Present and Future Plans: An Interview with Gary Snyder," in *Critical Essays on Gary Snyder,* ed. Patrick D. Murphy (Boston: G. K. Hall, 1990) 262.

3. Robertson 258.

4. Robertson 261.

5. Gary Snyder, *The Practice of the Wild* (San Francisco: North Point Press, 1990) 4. Subsequent page references to this edition are given in the text.

6. Tom Clark, ''Essays that Echo Thoreau,'' ''Book Review'' section, *San Francisco Chronicle* 16 September 1990: 3.

7. Clark 3.

CONCLUSION

As Gary Snyder begins his sixties, he shows no sign of lessening his contributions to North American culture and to international multicultural understanding. With all of his full-length collections of poetry and all of his prose volumes currently in print, Snyder has a substantial body of work before the public, and he continues to expand his readership. There is probably no other serious American poet writing today who is read more widely outside of academia than Snyder, and he is being read increasingly within the college classroom as well. In addition, *The Practice of the Wild* is attracting an entirely new set of readers, readers who will explore the poetry in order to learn more about Snyder and the ideas developed in his most recent volume. As the ecological movement nationwide and worldwide continues to grow, its participants will be searching out artistic representatives of their aspirations, emotions, and ideals. And Snyder speaks in a voice that they will recognize as one of their own. Snyder has already been recognized by the proponents of Deep Ecology, who generally treat him as their poet laureate.

As such readers learn about this poetic voice, they will have the opportunity to see that Snyder has produced a wide range of poems, diverse not only in techniques but also in themes. There is, of course, the major division between the short lyrics and the mythopoetic sequences. But there are the many lesser divisions between the simple, plain poems of everyday events and the elliptical, highly allusive ones about states of consciousness accessible only through ritual, discipline, and belief. There are also the various kinds of narrative poems focusing on the interconnected lives on this planet, as well as the political contradictions of public service, and the complexities of marriage and family. He has produced an impressive range of prose pieces as well.

Snyder's readers will also be waiting for the projects that he has promised to complete in the next few years. He has once more committed himself to finishing *Mountains and Rivers without End* and is actively researching material for additional sections. He is also working on another collection of prose, this one devoted to critiquing the limitations of Buddhism and Daoism in terms of developing environmental consciousness and ecological behavior. But writing, while it is Snyder's vocation, is not his life, and he expects to commit himself to significant ecological activism throughout the 1990s. As he told David Robertson, ''We seem to be on the edge of an era when the green movements will be the counter party to that of democratic capitalism, or at least the ecological and social conscience of democratic capitalism. So I expect that I will be engaged in the international green movement.''[1]

This does not mean that his future work will ignore or leave behind Buddhism. It remains an integral part of his worldview and his spiritual practice. Native American cultures and environmental practices also remain crucial for his views on right living. In *The Practice of the Wild* in particular, he demonstrates a keen ability to link what he has learned from Native American peoples across this continent with other inhabitory peoples around the world, such as the Ainu and Australian aborigines. Without ceasing to attend to the specific practices of such people, Snyder has gradually formulated a concept of international bioregionalism based on traditional and innovative practices of inhabitation and re-inhabitation.

Conclusion

Snyder has been recognized as one of the major American poets of the second half of the twentieth century. The increasing focus on ecology as a central concern of the American public will certainly affect his popularity as well as critical recognition of the significance of the issues he has addressed and the ways in which he has presented them. But since the problems he has brought to his readers' attention show no sign of abating, one can only hope that more readers will attend to the solutions he has proposed and the means by which to realize them. Snyder's poetry and his prose cannot afford to be read only to appreciate their aesthetic qualities. The message is too important to be ignored. Readers, unimpeded by the aestheticist limitations of some of Snyder's critics, may appreciate the full affective range of one of the most serious and intelligent American poets writing today.

Note

1. David Robertson, "Practicing the Wild—Present and Future Plans: An Interview with Gary Snyder," in *Critical Essays on Gary Snyder,* ed. Patrick D. Murphy (Boston: G. K. Hall, 1990) 261.

BIBLIOGRAPHY

I. Books by Gary Snyder

Poetry

Riprap. Ashland, Mass.: Origin Press, 1959.

Myths & Texts. New York: Totem Press/Corinth Books, 1960; New York: New Directions, 1978.

Riprap & Cold Mountain Poems. San Francisco: Four Seasons Foundation, 1965; San Francisco: North Point Press, 1990.

Six Sections from Mountains & Rivers without End. San Francisco: Four Seasons Foundation, 1965; London: Fulcrum Press, 1967; enlarged edition: *Six Sections from Mountains & Rivers without End Plus One,* San Francisco: Four Seasons Foundation, 1970.

A Range of Poems. London: Fulcrum Press, 1966.

The Back Country. London: Fulcrum Press, 1967; revised and enlarged edition, New York: New Directions, 1968.

Regarding Wave. Iowa City: Windhover Press, 1969 [limited edition]; revised and enlarged edition, New York: New Directions, 1970. London: Fulcrum Press, 1970.

Cold Mountain Poems: Twenty Four Poems by Han Shan Translated by Gary Snyder. Portland, Ore.: Press 22, 1970.

Manzanita. Bolinas, Cal: Four Seasons Foundation, 1972.

The Fudo Trilogy. Berkeley: Shaman Drum, 1973.

Turtle Island. New York: New Directions, 1974.

Little Songs for Gaia. Port Townsend, Wash.: Copper Canyon Press, 1979.

Axe Handles. San Francisco: North Point Press, 1983.

Left Out in the Rain: New Poems 1947–1985. San Francisco: North Point Press, 1986.

Prose

Earth House Hold: Technical Notes & Queries to Fellow Dharma Revolutionaries.
New York: New Directions, 1969; London: Jonathan Cape, 1970.
The Old Ways: Six Essays. San Francisco: City Lights Books, 1977.
He Who Hunted Birds in His Father's Village. Bolinas, Cal.: Grey Fox Press, 1979.
Passage Through India. San Francisco: Grey Fox Press, 1983.
The Practice of the Wild: Essays by Gary Snyder. San Francisco: North Point Press,
1990.

II. Archives

Gary Snyder Archives: Unpublished papers and letters. Department of Special Collections, University of California Library, Davis, California.

III. Interviews and Talks

Allen, Donald, ed. *On Bread & Poetry: A Panel Discussion with Gary Snyder, Lew
Welch & Philip Whalen.* Bolinas, Cal.: Grey Fox Press, 1977.
Faas, Ekbert. "Gary Snyder." *Towards A New American Poetics: Essays & Inter-
views.* Santa Barbara: Black Sparrow Press, 1979. 90–142.
Hertz, Uri. "An Interview with Gary Snyder." *Third Rail* 7 (1985–86): 51–53, 96.
McKenzie, James. "Moving the World a Millionth of an Inch: Gary Snyder." In
The Beat Vision: A Primary Sourcebook, ed. Arthur and Kit Knight. New
York: Paragon, 1987. 1–27.
O'Connell, Nicholas. *At The Field's End.* Seattle: Madrona Publishers, 1987.
Snyder, Gary. *The Real Work: Interviews & Talks, 1964–1979.* Ed. Wm. Scott
McLean. New York: New Directions, 1980.

IV. Bibliographies and Checklists

Kherdian, David. "Gary Snyder." In *Six San Francisco Poets.* Fresno, Cal.: Giligia
Press, 1969. 47–70. Includes useful biographical overview.
McNeill, Katherine. *Gary Snyder: A Bibliography.* New York: Phoenix Bookshop,

1983. An essential reference work; also contains valuable remarks by Snyder about various volumes.

V. Books on Gary Snyder

Almon, Bert. *Gary Snyder.* Western Writers Series 37. Boise, Idaho: Boise State University, 1979. A brief overview of Snyder's work up through *Turtle Island.*

Dean, Tim. *Gary Snyder and the American Unconscious: Inhabiting the Ground.* New York: St. Martin's, 1991. A psychoanalytic reading of Snyder in relation to the American frontier and the cultural unconscious of the mainstream population. Focuses on *Riprap, Myths & Texts,* and *Axe Handles;* downplays Buddhism and ecology.

Halper, Jon, ed. *Gary Snyder: Dimensions of a Life.* San Francisco: Sierra Club Books, 1991. Collects over seventy essays and reminiscences celebrating and commenting on the life and times of Snyder.

McCord, Howard. *Some Notes on Gary Snyder's* Myths & Texts. Berkeley: Sand Dollar, 1971. A valuable aid in reading *Myths & Texts,* with explanations and comments by Snyder.

Molesworth, Charles. *Gary Snyder's Vision: Poetry and the Real Work.* Columbia: University of Missouri Press, 1983. Analyzes Snyder's major volumes emphasizing political concerns. It contains valuable insights, particularly concerning *Turtle Island,* but is hampered by the author's unfamiliarity with Buddhism.

Murphy, Patrick D., ed. *Critical Essays on Gary Snyder.* Boston: G. K. Hall, 1990. Contains a bibliographical introduction; thirteen reprinted essays; four original essays by Lyon, Murphy, Yamazato, and Hicks; and an interview with Snyder by David Robertson.

Steuding, Bob. *Gary Snyder.* Boston: Twayne, 1976. The first full-length overview of Snyder's life and work. Although dated, it remains an excellent starting point.

White, Kenneth. *The Tribal Dharma: An Essay on the Work of Gary Snyder.* Llanfynydd, U.K.: Unicorn Bookshop, 1975. Mainly focuses on the idea of a new tribalism.

VI. Books with Chapters on Gary Snyder

Altieri, Charles. *Enlarging the Temple: New Directions in American Poetry during the 1960's.* Lewisburg, Pa.: Bucknell University Press, 1979. Compares Snyder with other American poets and argues that he writes in an "immanentist mode."

Castro, Michael. *Interpreting the Indian: Twentieth-Century Poets and the American Indian*. Albuquerque: University of New Mexico Press, 1984. Two chapters on Snyder defend his use of Native American materials and provide readings of individual poems.

Kodama, Sanehide. *American Poetry and Japanese Culture*. Hamden, Conn.: Archon Books, 1984. Extended attention to Snyder in terms of his being influenced by Japanese culture and experiences in Japan.

Kyger, Joanne. *The Japan and India Journals, 1960–1964*. Bolinas, Cal.: Tombouctou, 1981. Treats Kyger's marriage to Snyder and their experiences.

McLeod, Dan. "Gary Snyder." *The Beats: Literary Bohemians in Postwar America, Part 2. Dictionary of Literary Biography*, vol. 16, ed. Ann Charters. Detroit: Gale, 1983. 486–500. Particularly useful in terms of Snyder's relationship to the Beats and the San Francisco Renaissance.

Paul, Sherman. *In Search of the Primitive: Rereading David Antin, Jerome Rothenberg, and Gary Snyder*. Baton Rouge: Louisiana State University Press, 1986. Reflects on Snyder's major works and includes Snyder's responses to the interpretations.

VII. Critical Articles on Gary Snyder

Altieri, Charles. "Gary Snyder's *Turtle Island:* The Problem of Reconciling the Roles of Seer and Prophet." *boundary 2* 4 (1976) 761–77. Criticizes Snyder for shifting from the earlier role of seer to that of prophet based on an aestheticist argument.

Bartlett, Lee. "Gary Snyder's *Myths & Texts* and the Monomyth." *Western American Literature* 17 (1982) 137–48. Interprets this sequence using Joseph Campbell's Jungian monomyth.

Carpenter, David A. "Gary Snyder's Inhumanism, From *Riprap* to *Axe Handles*." *South Dakota Review* 26 (1988) 110–38. Criticizes Snyder for being misanthropic.

Crunk (James Wright). "The Work of Gary Snyder." *The Sixties* 6 (Spring 1962) 25–42. Rpt. in James Wright, *Collected Prose*. Ed. Anne Wright. Ann Arbor: University of Michigan Press, 1983. 105–19. First serious critical treatment of Snyder's poetry.

Bibliography

Folsom, L. Edwin. "Gary Snyder's Descent to Turtle Island: Searching for Fossil Love." *Western American Literature* 15 (1980) 103–21. Explores Snyder's recycling of American culture to its origins.

Holaday, Woon-Ping Chin. "Formlessness and Form in Gary Snyder's *Mountains and Rivers Without End*." *Sagetrieb* 5 (1986) 41–51. Analyzes Snyder's sequence in terms of the degree to which it is anti-teleological based on Buddhist notions of form and void.

Hunt, Anthony. " 'Bubbs Creek Haircut': Gary Snyder's 'Great Departure' in *Mountains and Rivers without End*." *Western American Literature* 15 (1980) 167–69. An excellent reading of one poem of this sequence, which is helpful for reading other sections as well.

Jung, Hwa Yol, and Petee Jung. "Gary Snyder's Ecopiety." *Environmental History Review* 14.3 (1990) 75–87. Focuses on the interrelationship of Snyder's ecological and spiritual beliefs.

Kern, Robert. "Clearing the Ground: Gary Snyder and the Modernist Imperative." *Criticism* 19 (Spring 1977) 158–77. Reads the early poetry as a reaction to modernism and a need for Snyder to shake off previous models to find his own poetic voice.

Lavazzi, Tom. "Pattern of Flux: The 'Torsion Form' in Gary Snyder's Poetry." *The American Poetry Review* 18.4 (July/August 1989) 41–47. Defines a poetics of internal tensions, particularly in relation to sexuality, and applies it to Snyder's poetry and consciousness.

Lewitt, Philip Jay. "Gary Snyder & The Vow." *Kyoto Review* 23 (Spring 1990) 1–17. Argues that Snyder's commitment to Buddhism results in his aesthetics flowing from his ethics.

Lin, Yao-fu. " 'The Mountains Are Your Mind': Orientalism in the Poetry of Gary Snyder." *Tamkang Review* 6–7 (1975–1976) 357–91. Treats Chinese allusions and influences in Snyder's work.

Mao, Nathan. "The Influence of Zen Buddhism on Gary Snyder." *Tamkang Review* 5.2 (1974) 125–33. Points out manifestations of Zen in Snyder's poetry.

Martin, Julia. "True Communionism: Gary Snyder's Transvaluation of Some Christian Terminology." *Journal for the Study of Religion* (South Africa) 1.1 (1988) 63–75. Details Snyder's rethinking of Christian terminology through Buddhist and ecological beliefs.

————. "Writing the Wild: Sunyata in Gary Snyder's Ecological Politics." *Proceedings of the Fu Jen University, Taiwan, Second International Conference on Literature and Religion*, forthcoming. Uses deconstruction to address the question of transcendence in Snyder's writing in relation to the Buddhist concept of *sunyata*.

Bibliography

Murphy, Patrick D. "Beyond Humanism: Mythic Fantasy and Inhumanist Philosophy in the Long Poems of Robinson Jeffers and Gary Snyder." *American Studies* 30 (1989) 53–71. A study of Jeffers's and Snyder's use of fantasy and horror in the service of anti-humanist and post-humanist philosophies.

——— . " 'A Mountain Always Practices in Every Place': Gary Snyder's Climbing Over Transcendence." *Proceedings of the Fu Jen University, Taiwan, Second International Conference on Literature and Religion,* forthcoming. Analyzes the relationship between Snyder's beliefs and a notion of transcendence based on Dogen's Mountains and Waters Sutra.

——— . "Mythic and Fantastic: Gary Snyder's 'Mountains and Rivers without End.' " *Extrapolation* 26 (1985) 290–99. Discusses "Bubbs Creek Haircut" and "Journeys" using Tzvetan Todorov's definition of the fantastic.

——— . "Penance or Perception: Spirituality and Land in the Poetry of Gary Snyder and Wendell Berry." *Sagetrieb* 5 (1986) 61–72. A comparative study of these two authors in terms of Berry's Christian-based beliefs and Snyder's Zen-based beliefs.

——— . "Sex-Typing the Planet: Gaia Imagery and the Problem of Subverting Patriarchy." *Environmental Ethics* 10 (1988) 155–68. Analyzes Snyder, Jeffers, and Berry in terms of the problems of gender-typing the planet as part of transforming culture.

——— . "Two Different Paths in the Quest for Place: Gary Snyder and Wendell Berry." *American Poetry* 2 (1984) 60–68. A companion to "Penance or Perception" focusing on their differing perceptions of place as wild and as cultivated.

Rehanek, Woody. "The Shaman Songs of Gary Snyder." *Okanogan Natural News* No. 19 (Summer 1984) 2–13. Treats *Axe Handles* in terms of the cultural function of poet-as-shaman.

Robertson, David. "Gary Snyder Riprapping in Yosemite, 1955." *American Poetry* 2.1 (1984) 52–59. Treats Snyder's development of his own poetic voice in 1955.

Shaffer, Eric Paul. "Inhabitation in the Poetry of Robinson Jeffers, Gary Snyder, and Lew Welch." *Robinson Jeffers Newsletter* 78 (October 1990) 28–40. Comparatively treats the concept of inhabitation as realized in the poetry of these three authors.

Shu, Yunzhong. "Gary Snyder and Taoism." *Tamkang Review* 17 (1987) 245–61. Explores similarities between Snyder's views and Taoism.

Williamson, Alan. "Language Against Itself: The Middle Generation of Contemporary Poets." In *American Poetry Since 1960—Some Critical Perspectives.* Ed.

Robert B. Shaw. Cheshire, U.K.: Carcanet Press, 1973. 55–67. Discusses Snyder and several of his contemporaries, and finds Snyder the most remarkable.

Yamazato, Katsunori. "A Note on Japanese Allusions in Gary Snyder's Poetry." *Western American Literature* 18 (1983) 146–48. Includes material gleaned from Yamazato's dissertation, emphasizing Japanese folklore sources.

Yip, Wai-Lim. "Classical Chinese and Modern Anglo-American Poetry: Convergence of Language and Poetry." *Comparative Literature Studies* 11 (1974) 21–47. A study of the influence of Classical Chinese poetics on Snyder and other American poets.

VIII. Dissertations on Gary Snyder

Jungels, William J. "The Use of Native-American Mythologies in the Poetry of Gary Snyder." SUNY at Buffalo, 1973. A detailed study of the Native American sources for *Myths & Texts.*

Krauss, James W. "Gary Snyder's Biopoetics: A Study of the Poet as Ecologist." University of Hawaii, 1986. Treats the ecological dimensions of Snyder's poetry.

Yamazato, Katsunori. "Seeking A Fulcrum: Gary Snyder and Japan (1956–1975)." University of California, Davis, 1987. The most sophisticated dissertation to date on Snyder's life and work, making extensive use of unpublished materials.

INDEX

Acts, 24–25

Ainu, 13, 160, 168

Allen, Donald, ed.: *The New American Poetry*, 45

Almon, Bert: on "Wave," 98

Altieri, Charles: on "Oysters," 88; "Six-Month Song in the Foothills," 78; *Turtle Island*, 129

Australian aborigines, 13, 159–60, 168

Bashō, 18, 102

Beats, 6, 11, 15, 43, 77, 109

Berry, Wendell, 139, 157

Blake, William, 104, 105, 128

Bodhissatva, 37

Brahma, 34, 97

Buddha, 36, 67, 75, 103, 119

Buddhism: 4, 8, 12, 13–15, 22, 28, 37, 44, 58, 59, 62, 66, 71, 74, 75, 76, 81, 83, 84, 86, 88, 89, 94, 95, 97, 98, 103, 104, 110, 112, 114, 119, 120, 125, 132, 140, 142, 150, 160, 163, 168; American Buddhism, 86, 143; Avatamsaka, 90 n.12, 94, 119, 142, 160; Chan (Ch'an), 14, 93; Dharma, 93, 103; Hua-yen, 69, 90 n.12; karma, 35; Kegon, 14,
90 n.12; koan, 7, 37, 83; kensho, 36; Rinzai, 13, 93; sangha, 14, 125; sanzen, 69; sesshin, 84; Shingon, 114; Shugendo, 114; Soto, 14, 93; sunyata, 74; tathata, 62; Vajrayana, 107 n.7; void, 29, 120; wuwei, 37; Yamabushi, 14, 161; zazen, 3; Zen, 4, 7, 13, 14, 36, 39, 40, 41, 71, 87, 93, 94, 95, 99, 128, 150, 163

Buddhist Peace Fellowship, 12

California Arts Council, 145

Castro, Michael: on "A Walk," 78; "Magpie's Song," 124; "What Happened Here Before," 126–27

Chen, Shih-hsiang, 136

Chinese poetics, 16–17

Christianity, 28, 48, 52, 58, 62

Chuang-tzu, 152

Clark, Tom: on *The Practice of the Wild*, 159, 161

Corman, Cid, 7

Coyote, 34, 37, 39, 42 n.20, 77, 117, 124, 132

Cummings, E. E., 15

Index

Daoism, 168
Dean, Tim: and order of publication of Snyder's works, 22; voicing, 33
The Diamond Sutra, 57–58
Diana, 24, 38
Dionysus, 25
Dogen: "Mountains and Waters Sutra," 160–61

Eliot, T. S.: 15, 22; *The Waste Land,* 22
Europa, 87
Exodus, 25, 161

Faas, Ekbert: quoting Snyder, 69, 72, 155
First Zen Institute of America, 6, 58, 71, 84
Folsom, L. Edwin, 117
Fudōmyō-ō, 114

Gaia, 15, 98, 138, 142, 143, 144, 145, 153 n.11
Gaia hypothesis, 131, 142
Gass, Alison (ex-wife), 3, 79–80, 82, 85
Géfin Laszlo: on poetics, 17
Genesis, 51
Georgelos, Peter: on Shamanism and Buddhism, 71; structure of *Mountains and Rivers,* 90 n.4
Ginsberg, Allen, 6, 8, 43, 68
Graves, Robert: *The White Goddess,* 4
Griffin, Susan: 18, 48; *Woman and Nature,* 48

Han-shan, 16, 43, 44, 45, 68, 77
Hicks, Jack: on *Left Out in the Rain,* 149
Hindu: 54–55, 87, 150; Hinduism, 22, 28; kalpa cycle, 28, 29, 41 n.11, 103, 152
Hsuan Tsang, 74

Hunt, Anthony: on "Bubbs Creek Haircut," 68

Indra's jeweled net, 12, 142
Io, 24–25

Japanese poetics, 16–17
Jeffers, Robinson: 3, 50, 61, 150; *The Double Axe and Other Poems,* 50, 61
Jesus Christ, 34
Jones, LeRoi, 7
Jung, Hwa Yol, and Petee Jung: on "Mother Earth: Her Whales," 120–21; Snyder's ecopiety, 129
Jungels, William J.: on *Myths & Texts,* 23, 25, 30, 31, 32, 34

Kanaseki, Hisao: on Miyazawa Kenji translations, 89
Keats, John: "Ode on a Grecian Urn," 29
Kerouac, Jack: 6, 57–58; *The Dharma Bums,* 6
Koda, Carole (wife), 11
Ko'kopilau, 73, 74
Kyger, Joanne (ex-wife): 7, 8, 10, 76, 82, 84, 86, 95, 130, 150–51; *The Japan and India Journals, 1960–1964,* 8

Lavazzi, Tom: on "Rainbow Body," 102
Lawrence, D. H., 3
Leach, Thomas: on referentiality, 52; "T-2 Tanker Blues," 62
Lenin, V. I., 112
Lu Ji, 136

Martin, Julia: on "The Bath," 113; "The Blue Sky," 74; Dharma and Vāk, 103; Gaia imagery, 143; "Little Songs for

Gaia," 142; structure of *Axe Handles*, 135
Marxist theory, 104, 112
McCord, Howard: on *Myths & Texts*, 25
McLeod, Dan: on Snyder's popularity, 9
McNeill, Katherine: quoting Snyder, 75
Milton, John: 52, 58; *Paradise Lost*, 51, 56
Miyazawa Kenji, 75, 89
Molesworth, Charles: on *Axe Handles*, 134, 148; *The Back Country*, 87; "Civilization," 106; long hair, 104; *Turtle Island*, 110, 118, 129
Muir, John, 36–37, 38

Native Americans: 53, 110, 111, 115, 157; beliefs, 77, 112, 121, 130, 159; cultures and societies, 4, 13, 28, 110, 128, 132, 150, 152, 168; myths and tales, 21, 22, 31, 32, 34, 77, 94, 112, 143, 164; rituals, 31, 32, 34; Alaskan Eskimos, 13; Anasazi, 88, 111, 112; Flathead, 31; Hohokam, 88; Hopi, 88, 111; Inupiaq, 158; Kwakiutl, 32; Salish, 31, 33; Sioux, 128
Noh drama, 66, 67, 70, 90 n.6
Norton, Jody: on "Burning the Small Dead," 79; "Six-Month Song in the Foothills," 77–78

Oda Sesso Roshi, 8, 76
Olson, Charles, 15
Olson, Ray: on *The Practice of the Wild*, 154
Oppenheimer, J. Robert, 82

Parvati, 68
Paul, Sherman: on "The Boy Who Was Dodger Point Lookout,"
79–80; inhabitation, 110; "Lookout's Journal," 94; *Myths & Texts*, 35, 39; *Riprap*, 44, 46, 59, 60; Snyder's response to Paul, 143; "Straight-Creek—Great Burn," 122; *Turtle Island*, 129
Petersen, Will, 6
Pound, Ezra: 3, 15, 17, 22, 136, 150; *Cantos*, 22
Prajapati, 34
Prajna Paramita Sutra, 73

Reed College, 2, 3, 149
Rehanek, Woody: on *Axe Handles*, 140, 144
Rexroth, Kenneth, 6
Ring of Bone Zendo, 14, 94
Robertson, David: on Snyder's vision, 155
Robbins, David: on "Burning Island," 101

St. Augustine, 62
Sakaki, Nanao, 8
San Francisco Renaissance, 6
Sarasvati, 97
Sasaki, Ruth, 6
Schelling, Andrew: on *Axe Handles*, 148
Schultz, Robert, and David Wyatt: on *Axe Handles*, 135; "Little Songs for Gaia," 142; "Money Goes Upstream," 147; "True Night," 141
Seami: *Yamauba*, 66
Shaman: 31, 35, 71, 124–25, 130, 131; shamanism, 30, 71, 74, 94, 112, 140, 149; shamanist, 143; shamanistic, 31, 33, 34, 35, 131
Shapiro, Robert, 127
Shinto, 160

Shiva, 68

Six Gallery, 6

Smohalla, 42 n.20

Snyder, Gary

Poetry

Axe Handles, 10, 134–48, 151, 154

The Back Country, 9, 10, 67, 75–89, 92, 93, 102, 130

The Fudo Trilogy, 9, 113

Left Out in the Rain, 10, 44, 58, 148–52

Manzanita, 109

Mountains & Rivers without End, 8, 10, 12, 63, 65–75, 99, 168

Myths & Texts, 6, 7, 12, 16, 21–41, 43, 47, 49, 51, 63, 65, 66, 103, 105, 132, 149, 161–62

A Range of Poems, 75, 89

Regarding Wave, 8, 9, 10, 16, 76, 96–107, 107 n.7, 113, 124, 141, 151, 161

Riprap, 6, 7, 8, 16, 17, 22, 41, 43–63, 71, 78, 79, 94, 113, 150, 162

Riprap & Cold Mountain Poems, 43–63

Turtle Island, 9, 10, 109–29, 130, 132, 134, 140, 146, 148, 151, 154

Six Sections from Mountains & Rivers without End, 65

Six Sections from Mountains & Rivers without End Plus One, 65–75

"Above Pate Valley," 53

"[After Rāmprasād Sen]," 87

"Alaska," 146

"All Through the Rains," 57

"Alysoun," 85

"Anasazi," 111

"Archaic Round and Keyhole Tombs," 99, 100–101

"Atthis," 149–50

"Axe Handles," 135–36

"The Bath," 113

"The Bed in the Sky," 102, 141

"Bedrock," 123–24

"Before the Stuff Comes Down," 105

"Beneath My Hand and Eye the Distant Hills, Your Body," 88

"A Berry Feast," 76, 77, 78

"Berry Territory," 139

"The Blue Sky," 65, 74, 124

"Bubbs Creek Haircut," 67–70, 73, 78, 89

"Burning Island," 101–2

"Burning the Small Dead," 79

"By Frazier Creek Falls," 119–20

"By the Tama River at the North Edge of the Plain in April," 97

"The Call of the Wild," 116–17, 124

"The Canyon Wren," 147

"Cartagena," 61–62

"Changing Diapers," 139

"Charms," 118

"Circumambulating Arunachala," 86

"Civilization," 106–7

"Cold Mountain Poems," 16, 43–45

"Control Burn," 115, 122

"Corn Maidens," 143

"Crash," 151

"The Dazzle," 124

"The Dead by the Side of the Road," 111, 113

"Delicate Criss-crossing Beetle Trails Left in the Sand," 140

"Dillingham, Alaska, the Willow Tree Bar," 146

Index

"Dullness in February: Japan," 150

"Dusty Braces," 111, 146

"Eight Songs of Clouds and Water," 98–99, 106

"Elk Trails," 149

"The Elwha River," 65, 70, 72

"Ethnobotany," 124

"Facts," 119

"Fire in the Hole," 79

"Fishing Catching Nothing off the Breakwater near the Airport, Naha Harbor, Okinawa," 140–41

"For a Far-Out Friend," 49, 54–56, 71

"For All," 147–48

"For the Boy Who Was Dodger Point Lookout Fifteen Years Ago," 79–80

"For the West," 87

"For/From Lew," 136–37, 139, 143

"Four Poems for Robin," 82–83

"Front Lines," 114–15, 116, 127

"Geese Gone Beyond," 144

"Go Round," 87

"The Grand Entry," 145

"Hay for Horses," 56

"Higashi Hongwanji," 59

"The Hump-backed Flute Player," 73–74

"Hymn to the Goddess San Francisco in Paradise," 71

"In the House of the Rising Sun," 97

"It," 104–5

"It Pleases," 120, 122

"It Was When," 102

"I Went into the Maverick Bar," 111, 113, 117

"Journeys," 72–73

"Kai, Today," 103

"Kyoto Born in Spring Song," 100

"Kyoto: March," 59, 60, 61

"The Late Snow & Lumber Strike of the Summer of Fifty-four," 46–47, 56, 162

"Little Songs for Gaia," 142–43

"Long Hair," 105–6

"Magpie's Song," 124–25

"Makings," 150

"The Manichaeans," 86

"Manzanita," 118

"The Market," 72

"A Maul for Bill and Cindy's Wedding," 145

"Meeting the Mountains," 105

"Mid-August at Sourdough Mountain Lookout," 45–46, 50–51, 153–54

"Migration of Birds," 57–58

"Milton by Firelight," 49, 51–53, 56

"Money Goes Upstream," 147

"Mother Earth: Her Whales," 120–22

"Mt. Hiei," 81

"Night Herons," 118, 120

"Night Highway Ninety-Nine," 70–71

"Nooksack Valley," 56–57, 58

"Not Leaving the House," 103

"O Waters," 125

" 'Out of the Soil and Rock,' " 149

"Out West," 81

"Oysters," 77, 88

"Painting the North San Juan School," 139–40

"The Persimmons," 151

"Pine River," 80

"Piute Creek," 49–50, 53, 54, 56

"Praise for Sick Women," 47–49, 54, 55, 71

"Prayer for the Great Family," 113, 117

"The Public Bath," 81

"The Rabbit," 98–99

"Rainbow Body," 102

"Regarding Wave," 103

"Removing the Plate of the Pump on the Hydraulic System of the Backhoe," 145–46

"Revolution in the Revolution in the Revolution," 104

"Riprap," 59, 62–63

"River in the Valley," 137–38, 141

"Roots," 102

"Seed Pods," 97

"Sestina of the End of the Kalpa," 152

"Six-Month Song in the Foothills," 77–78

"Six Years," 83–84

"Smokey the Bear Sutra," 9, 114

"Song of the Cloud," 99

"Song of the Slip," 100

"Song of the Tangle," 99, 100

"Song of the Taste," 100

"Song of the View," 100

"Source," 117

"Soy Sauce," 140

"Spel Against Demons," 113–14

"Steak," 111

"A Stone Garden," 59–61

"Straight-Creek—Great Burn," 122–23

"Strategic Air Command," 140–41

"T-2 Tanker Blues," 61–62

"Thin Ice," 56

"This Tokyo," 86

"Three Poems for Joanne," 150–51

"Through the Smoke Hole," 88

"To Hell with Your Fertility Cult," 85

"Toji," 58–59

"Tomorrow's Song," 125

"Toward Climax," 127

"True Night," 141–42

"Twelve Hours out of New York After Twenty-Five Days at Sea," 87–88

"24: IV:40075, 3:30 PM, n. of Coaldale, Nevada, A Glimpse through a Break in the Storm of the Summit of the White Mountains," 144–45

"Uluru Wild Fig Song," 146–47

"The Uses of Light," 118–19, 120

"Vapor Trails," 80–81

"A Volcano in Kyushu," 81–82

"A Walk," 78–79

"Walked Two Days in Snow, Then It Cleared for Five," 144

"Water," 53–54

"Wave," 97–98, 99, 102

"The Way West, Underground," 111, 112, 117, 130

"What Happened Here Before," 125–27, 128, 140

"What Have I Learned," 145

"White Devils," 97

"Without," 111, 112, 120

"Yase: September," 80

Prose

Earth House Hold, 9, 14, 76, 92–96, 99, 104, 105, 106, 129, 144, 154

He Who Hunted Birds in His Father's Village, 3, 21–23

The Old Ways: Six Essays, 9, 129–32, 142

Passage Through India, 8, 10, 130

Index

The Practice of the Wild, 9, 10, 154–65, 167, 168

The Real Work: Interviews & Talks 1964–1979, ed. Wm. Scott McLean, 129, 144

"Buddhism and the Coming Revolution," 95

"Dharma Queries," 95

" 'Energy Is Eternal Delight,' " 128

"Four Changes," 127–28, 154

"The Incredible Survival of Coyote," 131–32

"Japan First Time Around," 94–95

"Lookout's Journal," 94

"Now India," 130

"On 'As for Poets,' " 128

"Passage to More Than India," 95

"Poetry and The Primitive," 95, 97

"The Politics of Ethnopoetics," 131

"Record of the Life of the Ch'an Master Po-chang Huai-Hai," 93–94

"Re-inhabitation," 131

"Spring Sesshin at Shokoku-Ji," 95

"Suwa-no-se Island and the Banyan Ashram," 96

"Tanker Notes," 95

"What's Meant By 'Here,' " 128

"Why Tribe," 95

"The Wilderness," 128

"The Yogin and the Philsopher," 130–31

Story

"Coyote Man, Mr. President, & the Gunfighter," 152

Snyder, Gen (son), 9, 137

Snyder, Harold (father), 1, 27

Snyder, Kai (son), 8, 102, 103, 105, 136, 137, 150

Snyder, Lois Wilkie (mother), 1

Sokei-an, 71

Spretnak, Charlene: on valuing the female voice, 55

Steuding, Bob: on *The Back Country,* 76; *Mountains and Rivers,* 66, 71; "Not Leaving the House," 103; "Praise for Sick Women," 48; *Regarding Wave,* 97; "Song of the Tangle," 99

Tantra, 68, 90 n.11, 94, 99

Tarn, Nathaniel: on *He Who Hunted Birds,* 21

Thoreau, Henry David: 155; *Walden,* 24, 40, 94, 155

Uehara, Masa (ex-wife), 8, 76, 93, 96, 97–98, 99, 102, 103, 123, 140, 150

unsui, 99

Vairocana, 119

Vāk, 97, 103

Vissakamma, 67

Watts, Alan, 104, 127

Welch, Lew, 3, 135, 136–37

Whalen, Philip, 3, 4, 6, 43, 70

Whitman, Walt: 150; *Leaves of Grass,* 22

Williams, William Carlos, 3, 15

Williamson, Alan: on Snyder's achievement compared to his contemporaries, 89

Wright, James: on *Riprap,* 44

Yakamochi, 61

Yamazato, Katsunori: on arrangement of The Back Country

poems, 81; *Axe Handles*, 136, 138, 140, 141; Buddhism in U.S., 83; "Dullness in February: Japan," 150; enlightenment, 70; future efforts, 152; "Mid-August at Sourdough Mountain Lookout," 46; Regarding Wave, 100, 102; "Six Years," 84; "Spel Against Demons," 114; *Turtle Island*, 110; "The Uses of Light," 118–19; "Yase: September," 80

Yosemite National Park, 4, 5, 6, 49, 54, 59, 78

Yu, Beongchen: on Hsuan Tsang and Ko'kopilau, 74